Ulrike and Hans-Georg Preissel

Brugmansia and Datura

Angel's Trumpets and Thorn Apples

FIREFLY BOOKS

A FIREFLY BOOK

Published by Firefly Books Ltd. 2002

© 2002 Eugen Ulmer GmbH & Co.
© 2002 English translation David Bateman Ltd

Originally published: Germany: Verlag Eugen Ulmer, Stuttgart, 1997.
Original title: Engelstrompeten — Brugmansia und Datura.

First Printing

U.S. Publisher Cataloging-in-Publication Data
(Library of Congress Standards)

Preissel, Ulrike.
    Brugmansia and datura: angel's trumpets and thorn apples/Ulrike Preissel, Hans-Georg Preissel. — 1st American ed.
[96] p. : col. ill. ; cm.
Originally published: Germany: Verlag Eugen Ulmer, 1997.
Includes bibliographic references and index.
Summary: How to grow datura and brugmansia.
ISBN 1-55209-598-3 (bound) ISBN 1-55209-558-4 (pbk.)
1. Brugmansia. 2. Plants, Ornamental. 3. Gardening. I. Preissel, Hans-Georg. II. Title.
635.9/3395 21 SB413.B65.P74 2001

National Library of Canada Cataloguing in Publication Data

Preissel, Ulrike
    Brugmansia and datura: angel's trumpets and thorn apples

Translation of: Engelstrompeten
Includes bibliographical references and index.
ISBN 1-55209-598-3 (bound)   ISBN 1-55209-558-4 (pbk.)
1. Datura. 2. Brugmansia. I. Preissel, Hans-Georg. II. Title.
SB413. B76P7313 2001   635. 9'33952   C00-931520-9

Published in the United States in 2002 by Firefly Books (U.S.) Inc.
P. O. Box 1338, Ellicott Station, Buffalo, New York 14205

Published in Canada in 2002 by Firefly Books Ltd.
3680 Victoria Park Avenue, Willowdale, Ontario M2H 3K1

Visit our website at www.fireflybooks.com

Translated from German by Margaret Whale Sutton
Design by Errol McLeary
Typesetting by Jazz Graphics, Auckland, New Zealand
Printed in Hong Kong through Colorcraft Ltd

Front Cover and left: *Brugmansia* x *flava* 'Lilac'
description page 85.
Small photo: *Brugmansia versicolor* hybrid f. *plena*
'Charleston'
Back Cover: *Brugmansia aurea* 'Goldenes Kornett',
description page 81.
Following pages: *Brugmansia versicolor* 'Apricotqueen'
Page 2: *Brugmansia suaveolens* hybrid, very similar to
the variety 'Pink Delight'.

The authors are responsible for all drawings and
photographs unless stated otherwise in captions.

Preface

With the publication of the German edition of this book, we hoped as many gardeners as possible would become enthusiastic about growing *Brugmansia*. Happily our wish seems to have been fulfilled. And thanks are due to those plant growers who are successfully breeding this plant as a hobby. They have bestowed on us an ever more colorful and varied range of hybrids.

This has meant that the current varieties in this book have had to be revised. We have added a description of the numerous hybrids that *Brugmansia aurea, B. suaveolens* and *B. versicolor* have helped to develop. With the help of the publishers, we were also able to include the genus *Datura* within this edition. As a result, and because of the wealth of pictures, the book has not only considerably increased in scope but has also been enriched in content.

By presenting the old genus *Datura* and the more recent genus *Brugmansia* together, we expect to gain more acceptance for the genus name *Brugmansia*. According to the International Code of Botanical Nomenclature this has been a valid genus name since 1970, but in Germany and other European countries the genus *Brugmansia* (Angel's Trumpets) and *Datura* are often still not classified separately.

Unfortunately, the increase in the popularity of Angel's Trumpets has seen an increase in new diseases affecting the plants, some of which cannot yet be identified. The descriptions of both the diseases and their symptoms also had to be expanded. We hope that in the future those institutions that deal with plant diseases will give more attention to *Brugmansia* so that diagnosis and cures can be described in more detail.

In the chapter "Natural Changes in Angel's Trumpets" we mention some interesting features that make these plants so fascinating to observe.

We were able to gain totally new knowledge on *Brugmansia vulcanicola*. This was thanks to the help of Prof. Richard E. Schultes (Botanical Museum of Harvard University, Cambridge) and Prof. Alvaro Fernandez-Perez (Universitaria De Popayan, Colombia) who were able to obtain for us the rare seeds from their natural habitat. We would like to thank both them and the other botanists, gardeners and friends, Clarence Kl. Horich, Dr. Adolfo Holguín, Hans-Erhard Wichert, and Prof. Dr. Karl Zimmer, to mention just a few of the many who helped us in so many ways with the German edition.

Hannover, 2002
Ulrike and Hans-Georg Preissel

Contents

B. arborea hybrid 'Sternchen', descripton page 81.
Opposite page: *Brugmansia aurea* hybrid 'Citronella',
description page 82.

Brugmansia *and* Datura –
what is the difference?

*L*overs of imposing container plants are most familiar with *Brugmansia* and *Datura*. They know their marvelous flowers and their intense perfume. However, though the flowers may look remarkably similar, the plants themselves are actually very dissimilar.

For a long time, because of uncertainties, errors and mistakes in procedure, the scientific world has classified them together as *one* genus under the name *Datura*. Enthusiastic gardeners obviously found this confusing. The result was an array of popular names: Angel's Trumpets, Thorn Apples, Trumpet Tree, Tree Datura, and Tree Thorn Apple. All these names were used both for the varieties that grew like trees and for those that are like herbs.

As early as 1805 Christian H. Persoon, the botanist, considered the differences in the plant structures and the growth characteristics of the two types of plants to be so significant that he set up his own genus for all the tree varieties and

Below left: *Brugmansia* fruit never have spines. From left to right: fruit from *B. suaveolens* hybrids, *B. versicolor*, *B. x candida*, *B. aurea* and *B. arborea*. Below right: With the exception of *Datura ceratocaula*, fruits of *Datura* always have spines. From top left to bottom right: fruits of *D. metel*, *D. inoxia*, *D. discolor* and *D. ferox*.

Distinguishing characteristics of *Brugmansia* and *Datura*

	Brugmansia (Angel's Trumpet)	*Datura* (Thorn Apple)
Shoot	woody	herb-like, slightly woody only at the base
Size	trees or bushes up to 26 ft (8 m) high	large plants up to 5 ft (1.5 m)
Lifetime	long-lived, living for several decades	short-lived, mostly only one year or lasting longer because of storage organs under the ground
Length of juvenile period	relatively long; seedlings form their first flowers after numerous foliage leaves at about 2¹/₂ ft (0.8 m)	very short; under extreme conditions seedlings can form their first flowers right after the cotyledons
Formation and development of flowers	the individual varieties are affected by temperature	is affected by the daily amount of light (length of time there is light x the strength of the light)
Flower position	nodding to totally pendulous	upright
Fruit	berry fruit with no spines, pericarp fleshy, does not open during ripening	capsule fruit, mostly with spines; the chambers of the fruit open during ripening or fall at irregular intervals
Calyx	base does not widen out while fruit ripening	base grows while fruit is ripening into a cuff — *D. ceratocaula* is the exception
Seeds	with a corky seed coat; this is however not clearly distinct in *B. vulcanicola* and *B. sanguinea* without elaiosome*	without a cork-like shell; apart from *D. ferox*, *D. quercifolia* and *D. stramonium* usually has a noticeable elaiosome*

*Elaiosome: an easily recognized appendage on fresh seed. It is made of tissue that is rich in fat and protein and provides nutrient-rich food for ants. They thus take over the distribution of the seeds.

named it *Brugmansia*. The name "Thorn Apple", which was totally inappropriate, was dropped. Most of the herb-like annual plants have spines or hump-like fruits and in these cases the name "Thorn Apple" is very apt. All the tree-like varieties have smooth-skinned fruits which are often covered with velvety hairs.

Unfortunately, this classification did not last long. In 1833 Prof. J. J. Bernhardi, who was from Erfurt, Germany, began to doubt that the differences listed in detail by Persoon actually applied to all the tree-like varieties. He combined both types of plants again into the genus *Datura*. At the same time he did acknowledge there were differences and included a *Brugmansia* section within the genus. He also indicated that possibly this section would have to have its own genus once the characteristics of all the tree-like varieties had been described in detail. This was done in 1895 by G. Lagerheim, who once again elevated *Brugmansia* to the status of an independent genus. The uncertainty remained, though, for a long time. Until the present, the genus name of the tree-like Angel's Trumpets changed on several occasions. The various name changes are listed chronologically on page 13.

The *Datura* seeds, which are less than ¹/₂ inch (4 mm) in size, display a noticeable elaiosome when they are fresh. On the left, the black seeds of *D. discolor*, on the right, the brownish yellow seeds of *D. metel*.

Garden enthusiasts like treating the shrubby Angel's Trumpets (*Brugmansia*) as an independent genus. This has been the practice in the U.S.A. and Europe for quite a long time because it separates plants with very different growth requirements and totally different uses. While the *Datura* herb varieties are mostly annuals and are cultivated like summer flowers, all the *Brugmansia* varieties are used as container plants, at least in a North American climate. *Brugmansias* can be grown generally year-round in frost-free areas, e.g. in southern Florida and coastal southern California.

Tommie, Earl Lockwood, at the beginning of the 1970s in Ecuador. His doctoral thesis, which he completed at Harvard University, is considered to be the most comprehensive taxonomic description of the *Brugmansia* species to date. (Photo: A. Holguin.)

In 1973 T. E. Lockwood published what was the most thorough investigation of Angel's Trumpets. His results speak clearly for a separation of the species that grow like small trees and live for several years, into one genus, *Brugmansia*.

Since 1973 the International Code of Botanical Nomenclature has recognized this genus.

In German plant lexica, however, the common name *Datura* is often still used for both the herb and for the shrubby varieties. This leads to uncertainty when describing the plants and thus to confusion. It is not actually very difficult to distinguish the genera from each other. One distinguishing characteristic is sufficient to classify a plant into the correct genus (see table on page 11).

Chronology of the separation of the genus Brugmansia

1714 First illustration of an Angel's Trumpet under the description *Stramonioides arboreum*.

1753 Linnaeus classifies the plant as *Datura arborea* based on the 1714 drawing.

1805 C. H. Persoon collates all the varieties that grow into small trees and live for several years into a separate genus *Brugmansia* (named after Sebald Justin Brugmans, Professor of Natural History at the University of Leyden, 1763–1819).

1828 C. L. Blume uses the name *Brugmansia* incorrectly for a new Rafflesiaceae genus (*Rhizanthes* Dumortier, 1829).

1833 J. J. Bernhardi realizes that the differences listed by Persoon are not sufficient for separating out into a separate genus.

He classifies *Brugmansia* as a section within the genus *Datura* again.

1852 F. Dunal and ...

1892 R. v. Wettstein take over Bernhardi's classification and include Angel's Trumpets as a section of the genus *Datura*.

1895 On the basis of several years' research in Ecuador, G. Lagerheim collates the shrubby varieties into a separate genus *Brugmansia*.

1920 Because Blume (1828) had already used the name *Brugmansia*, even though he applied it incorrectly, C. van Zijp's opinion was that it could not be used again. He thought all the shrubby varieties should be separated off from the other types of *Datura*. He named the genus *Pseudodatura*. This is no longer considered to be a valid name.

1921 In a scientific paper on the genus *Datura*, W. E. Safford includes all the Angel's Trumpets.

1930 C. G. G. J. van Steenis refers to Persoon's initial usage of the name *Brugmansia* (1805) and declares that Blume's use of the name for the Rafflesiacea genus is invalid. Van Zijp's name *Pseudodatura* is also dropped. Van Steenis is in favor of separating all the shrubby varieties into one genus: he reverts to the name *Brugmansia*.

1930 P. Hochreutiner and ...

1943 H. U. Moldenke use the genus name *Brugmansia* for Angel's Trumpets.

1956 G. P. De Wolf, ...

1959 A. S. Barcley, ...

1965 S. Danert, ...

1966 M. L. Bristol and ...

1969 M. L. Bristol refers to Safford (1921) and regard all Angel's Trumpets as varieties of the genus *Datura*.

1973 T. E. Lockwood's comparison of the morphological characteristics of the herbs with the shrubby varieties clearly indicates that all the shrubby plants should be collated in one genus, *Brugmansia*. On the basis of this paper, *Brugmansia* is listed in most plant lexica as a separate genus.

Following pages: *Brugmansia insignis*, description on pages 34–36.

Brugmansia

Brugmansia — *The magical medicinal plant*

*I*f you want to research the cultural and historical origins of Angel's Trumpets, you will have to delve deep into the past. Since the Stone Age the ancestors of Inuit and American Indians have known how to use *Datura* to induce a change in consciousness. They used it in different rituals and customs. As the recipes for mixtures using *Brugmansia* have been passed down orally for generations, it is assumed that the South American Indians (e.g. Jivaro, Kamsa and Muisca) discovered these plants for themselves very early on. Whether, when they settled in the Andes, they noticed the great similarity between *Brugmansia* flowers and the *Datura* flowers which they were already familiar with or whether it was by chance, they recognized the strong hallucinogenic qualities of the Angel's Trumpets and used them freely. As early as 1589, reports on the Muisca in Tunja, Colombia, stated that:

"... a dead chief was accompanied to the grave by his women and slaves. They were buried at different levels all of which contained gold. So that the women and the wretched slaves were not terrified by the sight of their terrible grave before they met their deaths, the ancestors of the tribe gave them drinks containing intoxicating tobacco and leaves from the tree which we call Borrachero [= *Brugmansia aurea* or *B. sanguinea*]. They mixed these additives into their usual drink. In this way none of their senses could recognize the fate that was in store for them."

It would be wrong to say that *Brugmansia* was used solely as an anesthetic. This plant meant a great deal more to many Indian tribes. As they could explain the strong intoxicating effect which changed their consciousness only as the effect of supernatural, god-like powers, *Brugmansia* was considered to be a gift from the gods and accordingly was treated with great reverence. There were strict rules about the use of Angel's Trumpets — they were never abused as an intoxicant. Gustav Lagerheim was mistaken when, in 1895, he wrote the following about *B. sanguinea*:

"The tree is of little use, only the seeds occasionally play a role in the orgies of the Indians. According to Jameson, they cause an 'excitacion furiosa', so that I find it easy to believe that as the Indians have no brandy they put the seeds of the Huantuc (*B. sanguinea*) into their beer (chicha)."

Normally the aim and purpose of the *Brugmansia*-induced state was to make contact with the gods or the spirits of their ancestors. With the help of the gods and spirits, they tried to have a positive influence on their own future and that of the tribe. In an intoxicated state, they believed the level of consciousness achieved enabled them to ask for the help of the gods and to receive their advice. *Brugmansia* was the key that opened the door to this other world.

The importance placed on these plants in many South American countries was considerable. Alexander von Humboldt described Tonga (in this context he means the red-flowered variety of *Brugmansia sanguinea*) as the sacred plant of the sun temple of Sogamoso.

One reason why *Brugmansia* was not used a great deal as a hallucinogen was because of the extremely unpleasant effects of these plants. Those who had been affected by it told of terrifying visions of snakes and wild animals, of being extremely frightened and of after-effects that made them ill. For this reason the person who was intoxicated was always watched over by a "guard" who, if necessary, had to protect him from his own uncontrollable outbreaks of anger.

The Indians of Peru have another name for the plant. They call it Huacacachu, which means "plant of the grave". Many Indians believed that during a *Brugmansia*-induced state, the spirits of the ancestors would also give information about hidden treasures in long forgotten graves.

Until now not many people have been able to observe a *Brugmansia*-induced state. This is why J. J. von Tschudi's extremely detailed report from his notes on his travels in Peru during the years 1838–1842 is so informative:

"The beautiful red Thorn Apple trees (*Datura sanguinea*) grow at the river's edge ... on the less steep slopes of the mountain. The natives call them Huacacachu, yerba de Huaca or Bovachero and use the fruit to prepare a very strong narcotic drink which they call Tonga. Its effect is terrifying. I once had the opportunity of watching how it affected an Indian who wanted to communicate with the spirits of his ancestors. The ghastly scene is so impregnated in my memory that I will never forget it. Soon after drinking the Tonga, the man fell into a dull brooding, he stared vacantly at the ground, his mouth was closed firmly, almost convulsively and his nostrils were flared. Cold sweat covered his forehead. He was deathly pale. The jugular veins on his throat were swollen as large as a finger and he was wheezing as his chest rose and sank slowly. His arms hung down stiffly by his body. Then his eyes misted over and filled with huge tears and his lips twitched convulsively for a brief moment. His carotids were visibly beating, his respiration increased and his extremities twitched and shuddered of their own accord.

This condition would have lasted about a quarter of an hour, then all these actions increased in intensity. His eyes were now dry but had become bright red and rolled about wildly in their sockets and all his facial muscles were horribly distorted. A thick white foam leaked out between his half open lips. The pulses on his forehead and throat were beating too fast to be counted. His breathing was short, extraordinarily fast and did not seem to lift the chest, which was visibly fibrillating. A mass of sticky sweat covered his whole body which continued to be shaken by the most dreadful convulsions. His limbs were hideously contorted. He alternated between murmuring quietly and incomprehensibly and uttering loud, heart-rending shrieks, howling dully and moaning and groaning. This dreadful condition lasted for a long time until gradually the strength of the symptoms abated and peace was restored. Immediately the women hurried over, washed him all over with cold water and made him comfortable on some sheepskins. He then slept quietly for several hours. In the evening I saw the man again when, surrounded by a circle of attentive listeners, he was relating his visions and his talks with the spirits of his ancestors. He seemed to be very tired. His eyes were glassy, his body was limp and his movements were lethargic."

Brugmansia are rich in alkaloids.

After reading this impressive description of the different symptoms experienced during a *Brugmansia*-induced state, it is interesting to find out what these plants contain.

Like other weeds in the nightshade family, the *Brugmansia* are also rich in alkaloids. As well as tropane alkaloids, such as scopolamine (or hyoscine), hyoscyamine and atropine, Angel's Trumpets contain various related alkaloids of the tropane group such as norscopolamine and apo-scopolamine. By quantity, scopolamine is the most important. It makes up 30–60 percent of the total alkaloid content of 0.3–0.55 percent in the dried leaves, and as much as 80 percent in the *B. aurea* hybrid 'Culebra'.

Brugmansia use for medicinal purposes is still important in many Indian tribes.

In modern medicine the antispasmodic effect of these alkaloids has been well known for a long time. They form the basis for the most varied medicaments as, for example, spasmolytica. Although in the past *Brugmansia* were grown commercially for the production of hyoscine, nowadays mainly the *Datura* varieties are grown for this purpose.

The use of *Brugmansia* for medicinal purposes by many of the Indian tribes is still important. The Indians who live in the Sibundoy Valley, high up in the Andes, have remarkable knowledge of the medicinal uses of Angel's Trumpets. The various varieties cultivated by the Indians, which occur only there, and their uses, are discussed on pages 31–34.

Flowers and leaves of many different *Brugmansia* varieties are sold for medicinal use in the local markets in other Central and South American countries. In 1989 C. K. Horich, the botanist and plant collector, wrote about a dealer of medicinal plants in Costa Rica who, in addition to numerous prescriptions using Angel's Trumpets, gave him the following prescription on the use of *Brugmansia* flowers:

"*Brugmansia* flowers are used to treat varicose veins, both to reduce the swelling and to prevent them from spreading. Take four flowers and remove the stamens and pistils because these cause

Salvador Chindoy, Chief of the Kamsa Indians in the Sibundoy Valley, Colombia. Many Indian forms of the plant now originate in his garden. (Photo: A. Holguin).

allergic reactions. Boil the flowers in 1½ pints (1 liter) of water together with 1 teaspoon (5 mL) of menthol ointment, allow to draw for between one and two hours and then remove with a sieve. Preferably at night before going to sleep, rub the affected calves or legs with the tea-like concentrate and cover with bandages while they are still wet. Remove the bandages the following morning. Do not apply the lotion this day but wait until the evening of the following day. Any remaining liquid must be thrown away. On the fifth day, use four fresh flowers to prepare the liquid as before. Do not apply on the sixth day but repeat on the seventh.

This procedure must be carried out for a month, applying the lotion every second day.

Should the varicose veins reappear after a time, then the same procedure must be repeated for another month."

Unfortunately *Brugmansia* did not always attract positive attention. The unpleasant visions, which are the result of taking this plant, were explained as the effect of evil spirits. This soon gave *Brugmansia* the reputation of a dangerous, magical, narcotic plant which needed to be eradicated. Angel's Trumpets were often considered to be the home of evil gods: according to one legend, if someone inadvertently fell asleep in the shade of a *Brugmansia sanguinea* they would go mad. In addition, the belief that the poisonous *Brugmansia* honey polluted the whole honey harvest led to the eradication of countless Angel's Trumpets.

There is a real danger of fatal poisoning from using Angel's Trumpets.

The horror stories that have been published in the press on the dangerous nature of these plants unfortunately have not helped to present an objective picture of the very real danger of poisoning from using Angel's Trumpets. Reports often failed to mention that these were not inadvertent poisonings but rather conscious attempts to induce a changed state of consciousness. The dangers of doing this have already been discussed. Angel's Trumpets can pose a threat to children (because they will eat all sorts of things), even though their fruit do not resemble edible plants.

The *Brugmansia* might have long since been eradicated if it weren't for the fact that so many people are attracted by their ornamental value. These decorative plants, which are easy to cultivate, are finding their way more and more frequently into ornamental gardens. Depending on the geographical conditions they can either be planted out or used as container plants. It would be nice if this were one way of guaranteeing the survival of an interesting plant genus.

Form and structure of Angel's Trumpets

Understandably, a gardening enthusiast is mainly attracted by the flowers. But Angel's Trumpets are of interest in other ways. The structure of these plants includes notable features that will be discussed in the next few chapters.

Stages of development

In the following description the letters in brackets refer to features shown in the diagram on the right.

Immature stage

The first leaves that form after the seed has germinated display typical immature characteristics: they are comparatively small and do not have any indentations (**A**). A seedling has to grow to about 20 in (50 cm) before its leaves gradually assume the shape and size of the mature stage (**B**). In many varieties of *Brugmansia*, the change in shape can be seen in the incipient toothing of the leaves.

Even though the leaves are "adult" when the plant is about 20 in (50 cm) high, the seedling itself is still immature. The seedling does not reach the adult stage until it has set its first flower bud. This generally occurs when it has grown to between 2½–5 ft (80–150 cm). The first flower bud always develops at the tip of the shoot which then stops growing (**D**). This stop in growth marks the limit between the vegetative region of the plant and the flowering region which extends beyond it.

Mature stage

The seedling continues to grow by branching. As a rule, the two uppermost side buds sprout at the same time. The internodes, formed before the first flower bud, are so foreshortened that the side shoots seem to be growing at the same height. The result is a fork-like branching (in the diagram the left branching is only hinted at).

In the plant world, side shoots generally develop in the leaf axils. The *Brugmansia*, however, does not have any leaves directly where the branches fork. The leaves which should be here grow up to the side shoots. They give the false impression that they have sprouted on the side shoots (**E**) when in fact (from the point of leaf initiation) they belong to the previous shoot.

Once the plant has started to bloom, then new flowers continue to develop, provided environmental conditions are favorable. Each time the shoots stop growing, once two leaves have formed, a flower grows at the tip and new side shoots sprout.

A characteristic growth pattern develops that consists as a rule of forked and simple branching. The fork branchings have already been described. The simple branchings each have a larger and a smaller leaf before the final blossom. The larger leaf belongs to the previous shoot. It grows above

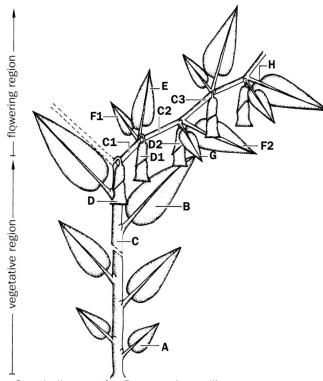

Growth diagram of a *Brugmansia* seedling:
A immature leaf
B mature leaf
C main shoot
C1 or **C2** or **C3** first or second or third side shoot
D blossom at the end of the main shoot
D1 or **D2** blossom at the end of the first or second side shoot
E leaf that was originally initiated before the blossom at the end of the main shoot. This leaf has grown further together with the new side shoot
F1 first leaf on the first side shoot
F2 leaf-bearing blossom at the end of the first side shoot has grown with the second side shoot
G first leaf on the second side shoot
H asymmetrical leaf blade from the flowering region

its shoot (where it originates) together with the new side shoot, so it looks as though it belongs to the latter (**E** or **F2**). The smaller leaf is always the first leaf to grow on the side shoot (**F1** or **G**). The second leaf which originated on this side shoot has grown together with the next side shoot and is moved onto it (**F2**). Because the internodes are severely foreshortened in the flowering region, it is very difficult to see how these leaves develop.

The same applies to simple branching on *Brugmansia*: the single side shoots that follow one after the other appear like a straight main axil that is unbranched, with flowers growing in the leaf axil. In fact, flowers on the *Brugmansia* always develop at the end of main or side shoots.

Up to six side shoots, each with flowers, can sprout one after the other out of the leaf axil in the flowering region if plants have been particularly well fertilized. These side shoots, however, are very squashed together and the leaves are very small. They give the impression that a whole bunch of flowers is growing out of one leaf axil.

Not only are the leaves formed in the flowering region smaller than those in the vegetative region, they also have a distinctive characteristic: the two sides of the leaf blades run unevenly down to the stalk, causing the leaves to develop asymmetrically (**H**). While the vegetation's points on the tip of the shoot are round and even, the leaf structures that lie along the side are oval and grow unevenly. Because the areas where the leaves grow are so cramped and restricted, the halves of the leaves develop unevenly.

When a shoot is changing to flower formation then it forms a subequal leaf basis. See the leaf on the left, the leaf under them is equilateral.

Shoots that develop close to the ground (as seen in the foreground of the picture) have to reach 3–6¹/₂ ft (1–2 m) in length before they begin to form flowers.

Construction of the flower.

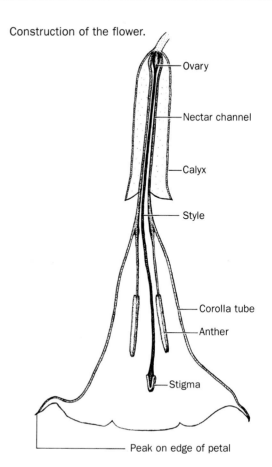

— Ovary

— Nectar channel

— Calyx

— Style

— Corolla tube

— Anther

— Stigma

— Peak on edge of petal

How the flower is constructed

Brugmansia branch not only in the course of flower formation as has already been described but also as the result of pure vegetative growth. They put out side shoots in the area close to the ground and make the plants bushy. Such shoots display characteristics similar to seedlings. They too have to reach a certain length before they can form flowers. Two important hints for cultivation:

1. Extreme pruning of the plants while they are over-wintering hinders the start of flowering in the next vegetative period.
2. Cuttings taken from the vegetative region flower later than tip cuttings taken from the flowering region.

The figure above shows the construction of the flowers. The individual petals of *Brugmansia* are normally fused, so the petals form the corolla tube, terminated by five "teeth" (see for example the flower of *B. aurea*, page 32). The *B. aurea* hybrid 'Culebra' is an exception. It has a very deeply-lobed corolla, being divided for approximately four-fifths of its length (see also pages 31 and 34).

The corolla folds over in the front along the edge of the petal. Along the edge of the petals there are pointed tips or peaks of varying sizes. These are the tips of the petals that have malformed into each other.

Up to half the filament can be fused with the corolla tube. As the corolla tube is very narrow at

B. suaveolens 'Weinstrasse', description page 88.

the base, the filaments that have fused with the corolla tube are jammed against each other. What are referred to as the nectar channels remain open in between. These lead to the nectar which is separated off at the base of the flower.

Normally the flowers of *Brugmansia* are made up of five parts: they consist of five petals with five points on the tips on the edges of the petals. Frequently, though, you can see flowers with six points and occasionally some with four on the same plant (see righthand flower in the picture above).

How to classify Angel's Trumpets

Typical characteristics that remain the same are used to classify individual plant species. It is not easy to find and describe these types of unchangeable characteristics on *Brugmansia*.

The growth form offers little help in this respect, for all the known types of *Brugmansia* are either perennial bushes or small trees whose form is not specific to a species.

Data on leaf shape, leaf size or furriness of leaves can often vary more within a species than between the different species.

Size and color of the flowers of a particular species can never be clearly described. They change so much according to the nutritional, temperature and light conditions that they can easily cross the boundaries into another species. Those flowers that are formed during the winter months, for example, are always a quarter to a fifth smaller than the summer flowers on the same plant. It is hard to recognize a *B. sanguinea* that, in summer, is tricolored (green base, yellow middle, ruby-red edge) then changes in fall as the temperatures go down into a two-colored form (green base and middle, ruby-red edge). It is not surprising that so many different names are in common use for a single species.

To take into consideration the many variations of one characteristic within a species, *Brugmansia* have to be classified without using the normal dichotomic (double-forked) keys.

It is more productive to compile a comparative list of certain characteristics that allow for over-lapping between the different species. The correct species of the plant under scrutiny can be found by using the column that has the most characteristics in common.

At this point we should mention the diverse propensity that *Brugmansia* has for forming hybrids between the various species. Unfortunately, it is just this property (which endears the plant to growers) that makes *Brugmansia* so difficult to classify exactly. The hybrid form, developing from two species, can display every imaginable variation of the characteristics it has inherited from its parent plant. The classification key describes only the intermediary type that occurs most frequently. In cases of doubt, therefore, the characteristics of the assumed parent plants should be taken into consideration.

The exact classification of multiple hybrids is even more complicated, as the characteristics often overlap to such an extent that it is no longer possible to give an exact classification.

Characteristics for *Brugmansia* classification

The following morphological traits have proven to be characteristic properties for classifying Angel's Trumpets, as they show a certain consistency even under changing environmental conditions.

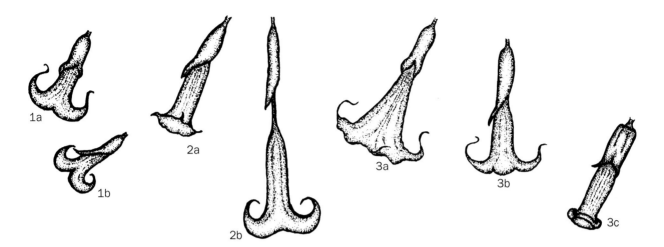

1. Opening of the calyx:
   a) calyx apex split in two to five "teeth", often of different lengths.
   b) slit on one side and the slit can stand out "like a horn" to the opposite peak or can be split further.

Unfortunately not all *Brugmansia* plants can be classified clearly into one of the two groups. In hybrids whose parents have different calyx forms, sometimes both forms of calyx openings will be found on one and the same plant. Even a wild species can be difficult to classify, as the teeth are often of such irregular depth that forms with several teeth can be wrongly identified as slit on one side with a split peak.

So far as is possible, a description of these species will see to this specific characteristic.

2. Narrowed part of the flower corolla at the end of the calyx:
   a) not visible
   b) visible
3. Form of the flower corolla:
   a) funnel-shaped
   b) trumpet-shaped
   c) tube-shaped
4. Length of the flower corolla
5. Length of corolla teeth
6. Anthers at the beginning of the flowering period:

a) glued to each other
b) free, not glued

The condition of the anther, whether free or gummed, must be examined immediately after the flower bud has opened. Anthers, which are gummed initially, as a rule become unstuck towards the end of the flowering period.

7. Shape of fruit:
   from egg-shaped to shaped like a spindle

Hybrids can display fruits of varying shapes, all of which are derived from the shapes of the fruit of the parent plants.

In addition to the hybrid forms mentioned in the classification key, there are further cross-breedings that in appearance differ so slightly from the "pure" species that only one parent can be classified with certainty (for example, *B. arborea* hybrid 'Engelsglöckchen').

By comparison, forms can develop within one species, presumably by mutation, which are so different from their normal form that the relevant species is almost impossible to recognize (for example, Indian forms of *B. aurea*). Examples of both possibilities are listed and described under the individual species.

8. Position of flower:

The opened flowers can take up a position that ranges from hanging horizontally to totally perpendicular. They never stand upright like the *Datura* species. Flowers that are inclined to hang downwards to some extent are described as nodding.

The position of a flower should be noted only on branches that are vertical or pointing upwards. On horizontal branches the flowers will almost automatically hang downwards.

Key for classifying wild species of *Brugmansia*

	B. arborea	B. aurea	B. insignis	B. sanguinea	B. suaveolens	B. versicolor	B. vulcanicola
Calyx opening	slit on one side	slit 2–5 times	slit 2–5 times	slit 2–5 times	slit 2–5 times	slit on one side	slit 1–3 times
Narrowed part of the corolla at end of calyx	not visible	not visible	visible	not visible	visible	visible	not visible
Shape of corolla	trumpet-shaped	trumpet-shaped	funnel-shaped	tube-shaped	funnel-shaped	trumpet-shaped	tube-shaped
Flower length	5–7 in (12–17 cm)	5½–12 in (14–29 cm)	10–16½ in (25–42 cm)	6–10 in (15–25 cm)	9½–13 in (24–32 cm)	12–20 in (30–50 cm)	6–9 in (15–22 cm)
Length of peaks on edge	½–1 in (2–2.5 cm)	1½–3 in (4–8 cm)	1–2 in (3–6 cm)	½–1 in (1–2 cm)	½–1 in (1–2.5 cm)	1½–2½ in (3–6 cm)	¼–½ in (0.–1.5 cm)
Anther	free	free	free — glued	free	glued	free	free
Shape of fruit	egg-shaped	egg-shaped	spindle-shaped	egg-shaped	spindle-shaped	spindle-shaped	oval
Flower position	nodding	nodding to hanging vertically	nodding to horizontal	nodding	nodding, sometimes horizontal	hanging vertically	nodding to horizontal
Peculiarities	furry style	leaves are often large		no scent calyx: inflated	calyx: prismatic at the base	flowers always hang vertically	fruit surfaces warty
Flower							
Fruit							

Key for classifying *Brugmansia* hybrids

	B. x *candida* (B. *aurea* x B. *versicolor*)	B. x *flava* (B. *arborea* x B. *sanguinea*)	B. *aurea* x B. *suaveolens*	B. *aurea* hybrid 'Culebra'	B. *suaveolens* x B. *versicolor* or B. *insignis* x B. *versicolor*	B. x *insignis* (B. *suaveolens* x B. *versicolor* x B. *suaveolens*)
Calyx opening	slit on one side	slit on one side	slit 2–5 times	slit 2–5 times	slit on one side (seldom several)	slit 2–5 times
Narrowed part of the corolla at end of calyx	not visible (seldom visible)	not visible	not visible	not visible	usually visible	visible
Shape of corolla	trumpet-shaped	tube-shaped	funnel — trumpet-shaped		trumpet — funnel-shaped	funnel-shaped
Flower length	9–13 in (23–33 cm)	8–12 in (21–30 cm)	9–14 in (22–36 cm)	6–9½ in (15–24 cm)	11–17 in (28–42 cm)	9½ in (25–40 cm)
Length of peaks on edge	½–2 in (2–6 cm)	½–2 in (2–5 cm)	½–3 in (2–7 cm)	1–2 in (3–5 cm)	½–2 in (2–5 cm)	1–2 in (3–6 cm)
Anther	free	free	free — glued	free	free — glued	free — glued
Shape of fruit	mixed shape	egg-shaped	mixed shapes	spindle-shaped	spindle-shaped	spindle-shaped
Flower position	nodding to hanging	nodding	nodding	nodding	usually hanging vertically	nodding
Peculiarities	known to have double forms	anther: often slightly furry		flower petals grow together only at the base		
Flower						
Fruit						

B. *aurea* x B. *insignis* x B. *suaveolens* x B. *versicolor*
The characteristics of the species involved in multiple crossbreedings overlap in such diverse ways that the classification key cannot be used (see page 91).

Wild species of Angel's Trumpets

Gustav Lagerheim (1895) in the 19th century and more recently Tom E. Lockwood (1973) are the leaders in research on Angel's Trumpets and their research forms the basis for the way the species is currently classified taxonomically. The following wild species can be differentiated:

Brugmansia arborea (Linnaeus) Lagerheim
Brugmansia aurea Lagerheim
Brugmansia insignis (Rodrigues) Lagerheim
Brugmansia sanguinea (Ruíz & Pavon) D. Don
Brugmansia suaveolens (Humb. & Bonpl. Ex Willd.) Bercht & Presl
Brugmansia versicolor Lagerheim
Brugmansia vulcanicola (A. S. Barcley) R. E. Schultes

Brugmansia arborea
(Linnaeus) Lagerheim

In 1714, in Père Feuillée's "Journal des Observations Physiques, Mathematiques et Botaniques" there was an illustration of the plant known today as *Brugmansia arborea* under the name *Stramonioides arboreum*. Based on this drawing, Linnaeus described it as *Datura arborea* in his botanical classification "Species Plantarum", which was published in 1753.

The name *Brugmansia arborea*, which is used today, was first mentioned by Lagerheim in 1895 in his "Monography of the Ecuadorean species of the *Brugmansia* genus". And although he was describing the white-flowered variety of *B. aurea* under this name (Lagerheim referred to the genuine *B. arborea* as *B. cornigera),* he is the author who classified *Datura arborea* into the genus *Brugmansia*.

Lagerheim was not the only person to make a mistake in the use of this name. Even today the most diverse species of white-flowering *Brugmansia* can be found in commercial plant nurseries listed incorrectly under the species description *arborea*. This is probably one reason why the genuine *B. arborea* is unknown to so many *Brugmansia* enthusiasts and is only seldom grown. Yet, this Angel's Trumpet is an extremely robust species that can resist both low temperatures and the occasional drought.

B. arborea originates from the Andes region of Ecuador, Peru, northern Chile and Bolivia. In its natural habitat it grows as a bush or small tree (*arborea* = like a tree). It prefers high altitudes, which are drier, between 6500–9750 ft (2000–3000 m). Periods of frost are not uncommon there. If the cold is too severe or if it is dry for too long, the plant loses a lot of leaves along with its younger, thinner branches. Once the unfavorable environmental conditions are past, this species sends out new shoots and continues to grow.

B. arborea is easy to recognize from the size of its flowers. They are the shortest of all the species

Opposite page: *Brugmansia arborea*

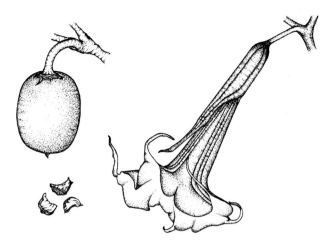

Brugmansia arborea: fruit, seeds and flower.

of *Brugmansia*. The trumpet-shaped corollas are between 4¹/₂–6¹/₂ in (12–17 cm) long, are white to creamy white in color and noticeably widen out to the edge of the flower. At the edge there are clear heart-shaped indentations between the turned-back peaks, which are approximately 1 in (2–2.5 cm) long. When viewed directly from below, these look like five-pointed stars.

During its vegetative period, *B. arborea* flowers evenly and constantly. Unlike other species of *Brugmansia* that flower in bursts, its flowers develop continually. This, plus the fact that the individual flowers have a relatively long flowering period of about four to six days (because of the stable nature of their corollas), means that during the summer months this Angel's Trumpet always retains the same appearance.

In their natural habitat the pendulous flowers are usually pollinated by moths. These are attracted both by the white color of the flowers and by the perfume that becomes stronger in the early hours of the evening. Even if *Brugmansia* flowers do not "emit the musk perfume of the night" (Vilmorin's *Blumengärtnerei*, 1896), the perfume, considered to be very intense and often almost intoxicating, does vary noticeably from species to species. In some cases it can help to identify a plant.

The corolla of *B. arborea* is tightly enclosed by the calyx, which is long compared to the overall size of the flower. In this species the tube-shaped part of the corolla, which is short and narrow, is almost always covered. The calyx, covered in velvety hairs, has a deep slit on one side. The elongated point, opposite to the slit, normally stands up like a horn, but occasionally can be split into smaller "teeth" (compare *Datura cornigera*, page 60). Frequently, the calyx falls off after it has been successfully pollinated. Sometimes some dried bits remain stuck to the developing fruit.

Leaf and flower stalks, along with the leaves which are wholly or partly dentated, are very furry. The young branches and leaves in particular are covered by a velvety, white down.

The egg-shaped fruit, which are also covered in velvety hairs, are, on average, 2 in (6 cm) long and have a diameter of about 2¹/₂ in (4.5 cm). Compared to other species, they are extremely plentiful on *B. arborea*. This increases the ornamental value of the plant. In the wild the fruit remain hanging on their stalks, which gradually become woody, until their outer tissues are completely weathered. During this time the fruit dries out and gradually becomes so deeply frayed from the effects of the weather that the flattened, trihedral (three-surfaced) seed can fall out. The seeds of *B. arborea* are large, about 4¹/₂ x 3 in (12 x 7 cm) in size, but have a thick cork-like shell that makes them light and able to be dispersed by the wind.

B. arborea is characterized by the white hairs on its style. All the other species of *Brugmansia* have smooth, hairless styles. Although it is not always as strongly delineated, this characteristic is also found in *Brugmansia* hybrids where one parent was *B. arborea* (for example, *B.* x *flava*).

Unfortunately this does not mean that all *B. arborea* hybrids have hairs on their styles. One particularly beautiful hybrid form, which is worthy of wider distribution, has a completely smooth style. Apart from this, it cannot deny its close relationship to *B. arborea*. These are the 'Engelsglöckchen' hybrids. They are very similar to *B. arborea* in their makeup and the way they grow, but they have a distinctly larger corolla (about 8 in [21cm] long), a flower edge that curves back and is more puffed up, and longer peaks (about 1½ in [4 cm] long) on the edges of the flower. In contrast to the wild species, these hybrids hardly ever bear fruit. Unlike the wild species, though, their abundance of flowers, even on smaller plants about 3 ft (1 m) high, and their dainty growth make them ideally suited for container plants in places with little space.

Brugmansia aurea Lagerheim and its Indian varieties

Brugmansia aurea was first mentioned in 1893 when Nils Gustav Lagerheim described it in an edition of "Gartenflora" under the title "a new golden yellow *Brugmansia*". Even then, plants of this species were being cultivated in the gardens of Quito, Ecuador, because of their extremely decorative appearance. The original habitat of *B. aurea* is at 6500–9750 ft (2000–3000 m) in the high Andes regions of northern Colombia, Venezuela and Ecuador. As this species of plant does not tolerate frost, it could never colonize the cooler and dryer areas of Peru and Chile.

The flowers of *B. aurea* are not restricted solely to yellow, as might be assumed from the name of the species (*aurea* = golden), but come in all the nuances from sulphur yellow through golden yellow to apricot yellow. It is not unusual to find creamy white and pink flowers as well. The trumpet-shaped flowers, which are from 6 in (14 cm) to a maximum of 12 in (29 cm) in length and of a firm, wax-like consistency, are brilliantly shiny where they widen out to the flower edge. If you look into a flower of *B. aurea*, you will be struck

Brugmansia aurea hybrid 'Culebra', description page 82.

by the five evenly divided nectar channels. These seem to be darker and they stand out clearly against the yellowish green base part of the corolla. The color contrast with the five freestanding brilliant yellow stamens in the middle is stunning.

The peaks are between 1½–3 in (4–8 cm) long. The flower edge between them can be both rounded and have slightly heart-shaped indentations. As the edge is normally tightly rolled back, this is not a major characteristic. The long peaks on the flower edge, on the other hand, are very distinctive. While still in bud they point forwards, then they curl in spirals.

Brugmansia aurea

B. *aurea* uses both its scent, which is particularly intensive in the early evening, and its brilliantly bright flowers to attract moths, but in its natural habitat, hummingbirds are often seen to be the pollinators. These birds find plenty of nourishment both in the nectar that is present in such abundance and in the numerous insects that are often trapped in the corolla tubes.

As on B. *aurea*, the tube-shaped base part of the flower corolla is completely hidden by the gleaming calyx with its thin covering of hairs. This is dentated two to five times, but one side has such a deep slit that it gives the impression of a calyx which is slit down one side with peaks that are further divided. Once pollination has been

successful, the calyx either falls off or remains on the elongated egg-shaped fruit like a dry skin. On average, the fruit reach a size of 4 in (10 cm) in length and 2 in (5 cm) in width. The outer skin remains on the tree until it has weathered, then the unevenly shaped seeds, which are less than $1/2$ x $1/3$ in long (12 x 8 mm), fall to the ground. The seeds are comparatively light, because of their cork-like deposits, and are spread both by the wind and by flowing water.

B. *aurea* is most distinctive because of its extremely imposing leaves. These are the largest of all the *Brugmansia* species. Depending on age, nutritional condition and variety, they can grow up to 28 in (70 cm) in length and 14 in (35 cm) in width. Normally these oval, lance-like leaves have a slightly wavy edge and in spite of being lightly furry, they glisten. In the past, presumably through mutation, new leaf shapes have developed whose characteristics vary considerably from the norm.

During tests using irradiated seeds a "normal" B. x *candida* developed among the other young plants. Its leaf shape was similar to the Indian

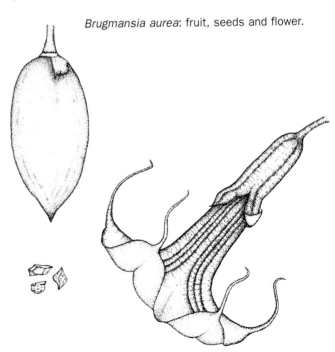

Brugmansia aurea: fruit, seeds and flower.

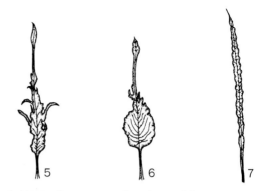

type 'Quinde', which reinforces the assumption that mutations are responsible for the changes in leaf shape. As has already been mentioned, the Indians who live in the Sibundoy Valley in Colombia gathered those plants whose leaf shape, color or size differed from those of the wild variety. As they used mainly the leaves of the *Brugmansia* plants for their own purposes, they selected their plants more for leaf changes than for flowers. These plants were then propagated exclusively vegetatively from large pieces of stem. Horticulturists adopted the terms used by the Indians to describe the various plants, most of which were developed from *B. aurea* types, and used them as names for the different varieties. If you take their flower characteristics into consideration, then other wild species could have played a part in the development of some of the varieties listed in the following table. 'Quinde' or 'Ocre' are two possibilities — which is why when they are cultivated they are also described as *B. x candida*.

Various Indian varieties and how they are used medicinally by the Indians

(Illustrations and text from Bristol, 1969, with alterations.)

'**Amaron**' (1) Widespread; its leaves were used to treat sepsis and to alleviate rheumatic pains.

'**Biangan**' (2) Indian name for the varieties of *B. x candida* that were widespread. Leaves and flowers were pounded and mixed with the feed given to hunting dogs before the start of a hunt so that they would be better able to scent game.

'**Buyes**' (3) Indian name for the wild species of *B. aurea*. Its leaves were pounded to powder and used to alleviate rheumatic pains.

'**Munchira**' (4) Rare. Its tiny, highly poisonous leaves were used to treat rheumatic pains, infestations of worms and as an emetic. It was also used to treat erysipelas (a streptococcal infection).

'**Quinde**' (5) Best known of all the commercially used varieties. An infusion prepared from its leaves was used both against rheumatic pains and to treat infestations of worms. The leaves were applied to treat sepsis. Leaves, and sometimes flowers as well, were used for their hallucinogenic properties.

'**Salaman**' (6) The rarest variety, only known from one habitat. Its owner used the leaves along with those of 'Quinde' and 'Culebra' to produce an infusion to bathe limbs and joints that were affected by rheumatism.

'**Culebra**' (7) Previous varieties have been relatively easy to identify as *Brugmansia*, but in 1942 a plant was discovered in the Sibundoy Valley that apparently could not be classified in this genus.

Its nodding to pendulous flowers, which were greenish white and 6–9½ in (15–24 cm) long, were so deeply split between the peaks on the edge (three- to four-fifths of the whole length) that they gave the impression of five individual flower petals. The gleaming calyx had almost no hairs and lay tightly around the flower corolla. Only the three to four "teeth" that were produced by the slit at the mouth seemed to be inflated. The

33

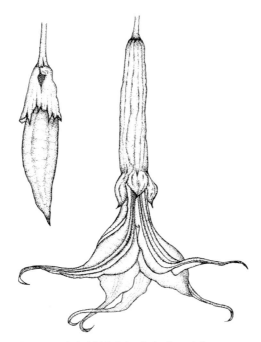

Brugmansia aurea hybrid 'Culebra': fruit and flower

leaves were up to 12 in (30 cm) in length. They had an undulated rim, were about ¹/₂ in (1.5 cm) wide at the broadest point and the leaf blade was reduced almost to the middle rib.

An important feature of this variety, which was described by R. E. Schultes in 1955 as *Methisticodendron amesianum*, was that the pistil was made up of several individual styles. This distinctive pistil was not found in any other *Brugmansia*. According to Schultes, each pistil consists of three styles. Each pistil is independent of the other and each has an undivided stigma. As well as these "triple varieties" there are flowers whose pistils consist of two styles that are glued together. Both types of pistil are frequently seen on one and the same plant. Lockwood (1973) classified *Methisticodendron amesianum* into the genus *Brugmansia*. It is considered to be one of the most interesting mutation types and is assumed to have developed from a *B. aurea* hybrid. Its elongated oval shape seems to confirm this assumption, as it is very different from the normal fruit shape of a *B. aurea*.

The name given to the variety is 'Culebra', which is the translation of the description "mutscuai borrachero" used by the Kamsa Indians. The most literal translation would be "plant of the snake that intoxicates or makes drunk". The term "snake" probably refers to the long, narrow leaf shape of this *Brugmansia*.

In earlier times, because the properties of this plant caused such a major change in consciousness, it was used for prophecy and for learning magical arts. Novices could only be initiated into the secrets of the cult during a state of intoxication. Even today, the Indians prepare an infusion from the leaves to relieve rheumatic pains.

Brugmansia insignis (Rodrigues) Lagerheim

In 1891 B. Rodrigues described a plant that was discovered in the Upper Amazon region of Peru as *Datura insignis*. Just four years later, G. Lagerheim listed a very similar species in his comprehensive monograph and gave it the species sub-name "longifolia" because of its long, narrow leaves. It seems quite probable that *Brugmansia insignis* and *B. longifolia* are the same plant species. The distinctive funnel shape of the flowers with their relatively long, narrowed part of the corolla tube would seem to corroborate this. These characteristics can be clearly seen on a photograph of the holotype that Lagerheim deposited in the Botanical Garden in Berlin. Unfortunately, Lagerheim's herbarium material was destroyed in World War II, so there is no proof to support this assumption. As the previous description with the sub-species name of "insignis" has priority anyway, according to the international rules of nomenclature, this can easily be overcome.

T. E. Lockwood, in his revision of the genus *Brugmansia*, questioned the status of *B. insignis*. In the American plant lexicon "Hortus Third"

At first glance, the flowers of *Brugmansia suaveolens* (left) and *B. insignis* (right) look similar. *B. insignis* is easily recognizable by the longer thread-shaped flower peaks that are usually bent forwards. The narrowed parts of the flower corollas are also distinctly longer.

1976, he finally classified *B. insignis* as a natural hybrid: *B.* x *insignis* (Rodrigues) Lockwood ex Davis is supposed to have developed from the second generation of a cross between *B. suaveolens* and *B. versicolor* and then a cross-back with *B. suaveolens*. In 1983, after Lockwood's untimely death, Davis published this new combination in accordance with the international rules of nomenclature.

We have, however, not been able to confirm Lockwood's result in our extensive crossbreeding experiments. There were strong variations in the flower characteristics of all the seedlings, but they were always within the characteristics of the parent plants, *B. suaveolens* and *B. versicolor*. Crossings of different plants of *B. insignis* with each other produced a very unified progeny where the shape of the leaves, flowers and even fruit was typical of *B. insignis*. Uniform progeny is an indisputable indicator of an independent species. The fact that *B. insignis* exceeds all the other species of *Brugmansia* in its need for warmth speaks against its evolution as the result of hybridization.

The hybridization procedure described by Lockwood (*B. suaveolens* x *B. versicolor*) x *B. suaveolens* seems to be too complicated to have taken place repeatedly in nature. According to observations made by A. Holguin, the Ecuadorean expert on Angel's Trumpets, *B. insignis* has its natural range in the lower mountain zone of the eastern Andes of Peru and is thus separated spatially both from *B. versicolor* and from *B. suaveolens*.

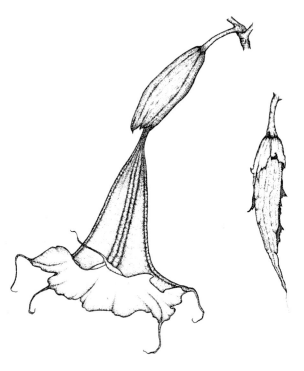

Brugmansia insignis: flower and fruit.

B. insignis has relatively thin, brittle branches. Its scented flowers are 10–16 in (25–40 cm) long and narrowed to a thin long tube in the base section, that is clearly visible outside the calyx. The adjoining part of the flower corolla is distinctly funnel-shaped and has petal edges that are 1–2$\frac{1}{3}$ in (3–6 cm) long, and often twisted in spirals. The funnel shape of the flower corolla and the fact that the petal edges are very thin and curved slightly forwards are two of the most distinctive characteristics of *B. insignis*.

Because the corolla tends to be very thin in texture, the flowers open completely only when the air humidity is high, which is regularly during the morning hours. During the midday heat the flower corollas tend to hang down limply and look slightly folded together. In their natural position the flowers are horizontal to slightly nodding.

The flowers can be cream, white and varying shades of pink. The anthers are slightly glued together when the flower opens, but then quickly open from the pressure of the filaments.

Like most Angel's Trumpets, *B. insignis* flowers in bursts. The higher the average daily temperature is, the less clearly the different growth phases are delineated. This shows how important warmth is for this Angel's Trumpet. In its tropical homeland it truly deserves its given name "insignis" (*insignis* = strikingly beautiful). In central Europe we see it at its full beauty only during a particularly hot summer. The calyx is 5$\frac{1}{2}$–6$\frac{1}{4}$ in (14–16 cm) long and has 2–5 teeth. It is shaped by the calyx veins that are very prominent, and never lies tightly along the corolla tube. The narrowish, sword-shaped leaves have smooth edges and are always shining. The fruits, which are known in cultivation only from artificial pollination, are noticeably narrow and strongly furrowed.

The few places where *B. insignis* grows in the wild are on the eastern side of the Peruvian and Ecuadorean Andes. It seldom sets fruit in nature and there is a real danger that this plant will die out. The indication is that *B. insignis* — the strikingly beautiful — owes its survival exclusively to its extremely ornamental value. This is why people have cultivated it, and have planted it next to their houses and along their streets.

Brugmansia sanguinea (Ruíz & Pavon) D. Don

This plant was first described as *Datura sanguinea* in 1799 when it was mentioned by Ruíz and Pavon in a collection of Peruvian and Chilean flora. Its name was changed to *Brugmansia sanguinea* in 1835.

This extremely robust Angel's Trumpet is found along the mountain slopes of the Andes from northern Colombia to northern Chile at altitudes of 6500–9750 ft (2000–3000 m). *B. sanguinea* usually tolerates the light frosts that occur frequently in these regions. If the periods of frost are too long or too cold, then the plants lose their leaves and branches and freeze back into the wood. In the next vegetation period they produce new shoots without any difficulty from the surviving plant stalks.

B. sanguinea is easy to recognize from the shape of its flowers. The corolla is tube-shaped and widens out only at the mouth opening. The prominent yellowish green flower veins, which are furry, give the corolla a stability no other Angel's Trumpet has. The flower edge curves back as if it has been rolled. It ends in peaks about ½–1 in (1–2 cm) long that curve back. In this species, the length of the flower can be from 6–10 in (15–25 cm), depending on the variety.

B. sanguinea is the most wonderfully colored of all the Angel's Trumpets. While pastel-colored corollas dominate in the other species, these plants have intense shining colors or combinations of colors. There are multicolored forms with a green flower base, yellow or cream-colored middle, and red or orange mouth found, as well as single-colored forms whose flowers are colored a brilliant red, pink, orange, golden yellow or light yellow. No white-flowered plants, however, have been found. The variety and the prevalent temperatures have a major effect on the coloring of individual flowers. Thus, a plant that is tricolored (green/yellow/reddish orange) in summer when the temperature is about 68°F (20°C), will become two-colored (green/ruby red) in fall when the temperature is about 50°F (10°C). A plant that in summer has brilliant yellow flowers will have greenish yellow flowers in fall.

Very warm summer months can unleash veritable explosions of color in the other species of *Brugmansia*, but plants of *B. sanguinea* will have no flowers at all. This is mainly due to temperature conditions. In this species, temperatures above 71°F (22°C) seem to inhibit flower development. New buds do continue to form, but

Single-colored, yellow-flowered example of *Brugmansia sanguinea.*

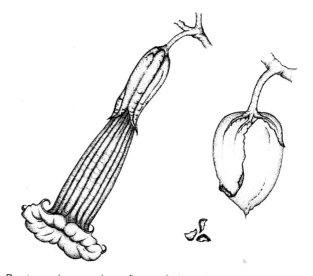

Brugmansia sanguinea: flower, fruit and seeds.

37

when the temperatures are high, the buds only reach an average size of about ¹/₂ in (1 cm) before they dry off and fall. Where the average temperature is 50°–60°F (10°–16°C), on the other hand, flower development is expected to be good. This is what makes this Angel's Trumpet ideally suited to be a greenhouse plant. It will flower there for almost the whole winter.

The leaves, which range from egg-shaped to spear-like, have a wavy, indented edge and definitely add ornamental value. They are covered in soft hairs, as are the young branches and the corollas of the flowers. The corollas are split at their mouths two to five times and look "puffed up" because their veins stand out so clearly. After successful pollination the corolla continues to increase in size. It sticks to the egg-shaped fruit and envelops it while the fruit is ripening.

In their native habitat *B. sanguinea* are pollinated by hummingbirds. These Angel's Trumpets show just how well a plant can be attuned to the abilities and characteristics of its pollinator. Hummingbirds have a well-developed sense of perception within the red spectrum. *B. sanguinea* flowers often have brilliant red corolla sections (*sanguinea* = red like blood). Hummingbirds have a weak sense of smell. Of all the species of *Brugmansia*, *B. sanguinea* are the only ones to have no scent.

These Angel's Trumpets also use animals to spread their seeds. The fruit, which is furry, is about 3 in (8 cm) long and 2 in (5 cm) wide. It does not dry out like those of the other species. Either it rots on the tree and the seed enclosed within germinates in the fruit or empty, opened fruit are found hanging on the trees. This happens frequently in their native habitats. During a botanical expedition in 1892, almost all the ripe fruit found hanging on the *B. sanguinea* trees had

Opposite page: Tricolored example of *Brugmansia sanguinea*.

Multicolored flowers of *Brugmansia sanguinea*. The flowers on the left have yellow in the middle and those on the right are cream-colored.

large round openings in their sides. The seed had either been taken out or had fallen out. Birds or bats were assumed to be responsible, but no creature was ever caught in the act.

In this context it is interesting that *B. sanguinea* does not contain a large proportion of cork compared to the other species. In size it is considerably heavier than the other *Brugmansia* seeds and can only depend on the wind for dissemination to a very limited extent.

Except for the forms of *B. aurea* already discussed, *B. sanguinea* is the Angel's Trumpet used most frequently by the Indians for medicinal purposes. Its Indian name is "Guamuco" or "Guamucu borrachera". A mixture of the flowers of *B. sanguinea* with leaves from the *B. aurea* hybrid 'Culebra' and the leaves of a stinging nettle weed are said to help ease rheumatic pains.

Brugmansia suaveolens (Humb. & Bonpl. ex Willd.) Bercht & Presl

This Angel's Trumpet, first described by Willdenow in 1809 as *Datura suaveolens,* was discovered by Alexander von Humboldt and Aimé Bonpland (1799–1804) on their now famous voyage to North America. It was classified into the genus *Brugmansia* in 1823.

These Angel's Trumpets are probably nowadays the most widespread of all. They originally came from the coastal regions of the rainforest of southeast Brazil. There they grow below 3500 ft (1000 m) on the flats, preferably at the edges of the forest or along the river banks where humidity, temperatures and rainfall are all high.

The ornamental value of these plants was recognized very early on and as a result people began to cultivate them. Nowadays, *B. suaveolens* is found in Brazil and in most other parts of South America, in Mexico, on the Caribbean Islands, and also in tropical Africa.

In Europe this large-flowered variety with its abundant flowers soon became very well known as a container plant. Most of the *Brugmansia* which are currently in cultivation are probably *B. suaveolens* or one of its hybrids.

This species of plant has a typical flower shape. The corolla tube is constricted as it exits the calyx then widens out evenly to the flower edge. The result is a funnel shape. The peaks on the flower's edge are always short, usually only $1/2$–1 in (1–2.5 cm) long and curved outwards. They are never rolled back.

Normally each flower has five peaks on its edge. Each of these is supported by three prominent flower veins. This produces the corolla shape that is typical of the species. There are frequent examples of *B. suaveolens* that produce flowers with four, five or six peaks on the same plant. The edge of the openings at their mouths is enlarged by or decreased by a fifth because of the segment that is either added or removed. These flowers will also have four, five or six stamens, respectively. What causes these numerical variations in the flower parts is still unclear.

In all the varieties of *B. suaveolens* the anthers are glued to each other after the flower buds open. They form a unit that only begins to loosen during flowering. In other species the anthers are already visible and are independent and free. This is a sure sign for identifying *B. suaveolens*. In some hybrids the anther is slightly glued or only

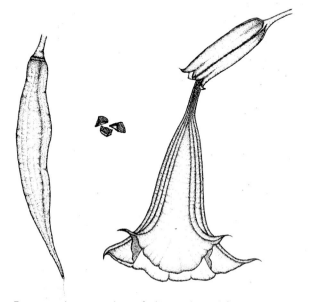

Brugmansia suaveolens: fruit, seeds and flower.

partly glued. This is proof that *B. suaveolens* has played a part in the development of the hybrid form.

The flower corollas of *B. suaveolens* are 9½–13 in (24–32 cm) long. They are mainly white or creamy white in color, but occasionally yellow or pink. These gleaming bright flower colors, the scent, which is intense in the evening (*suaveolens* = fragrant), and, not least, the pendulous to horizontal position of the flowers indicate that night moths are the probable pollinators.

The way the position of the flower changes from bud to full bloom is an interesting characteristic of these Angel's Trumpets: it is because of the increasing weight of the flower! The young bud grows to a size of about 1 in (2 cm) in an upright to slightly nodding position. During its next growth stage the flower stalk bends until, when the flower bud is about 2½ in (7 cm) in size, it is hanging almost perpendicular. Then the stalk adjusts itself upwards again and by the time of flowering it is often horizontal. After pollination, the flower stalk, which is still growing, is bent downwards by the increasing weight of the fruit.

B. suaveolens flowers in bursts. It has one flowering phase which can last from two to four weeks. This is followed by a period during which the plants set new flower buds and create the prerequisite for a new burst of flowers; however, *B. suaveolens* is never completely without flowers as are some of the other species. The growth rhythm can often only be observed by the change between strong-flowering and weak-flowering phases.

If the light conditions are sufficient and the temperatures are between 53°–64°F (12°–18°C), this Angel's Trumpet will flower even during winter (in temperate climates). It is therefore particularly well-suited for growing in greenhouses.

B. suaveolens is one of the strongest-growing species of this genus. In its natural habitat, it grows into a bush, and sometimes into a small tree, up to a height of 10½–17½ ft (3–5 m).

Brugmansia suaveolens grown as a standard.

The leaves are oval to elliptical in shape. They gleam, are whole and have hardly any hairs. The calyx, which is also gleaming and almost hairless, looks angular — almost prismatic — at the base and slightly puffed up because of the prominent calyx veins. At the mouth it splits into two to five "teeth" usually of the same length. After successful pollination it often sticks to the developing fruit and envelops it as a dry, paper-like layer.

The elongated fruit are shaped like spindles, 4–8½ in (10–22 cm) long. In spite of their shining surface, they have numerous uneven patches and furrows. In nature, like most of the species of *Brugmansia*, they dry out while still on the tree so that the seed is released only after the outer skin has weathered. The seed is tiny (about ¼ in [8 mm] in size) and is naturally disseminated by wind or flowing water.

Along with *B. x candida*, *B. suaveolens* is the Angel's Trumpet most widely cultivated. It grows well, starts to fork early and its foliage is neat and tends to cover it from top to bottom. These factors, plus its ability to flower relatively independently of the weather, are all contributing factors in its popularity.

Unfortunately, it is just this species that is attacked by the most diverse kinds of leaf pests. Their damage profiles and the ways of combating these are listed on pages 98–103.

Brugmansia versicolor
Lagerheim

B. versicolor was recognized in 1895 by Nils Gustav Lagerheim as an independent species and described, under the name it still bears, in the "Monography of the Ecuadorean Species of the Genus *Brugmansia*".

Its habitat is restricted to the tropical regions of Ecuador, where it grows within the Guayaquil Basin and south of the Gulf of Guayaquil on the flat up to an altitude of 2600 ft (750 m). Within this relatively small distribution area, it produces a wide variation in flower size and furriness. The plants with the largest flowers have been seen in the northern regions, while the furriest ones with distinctly small flowers were in the southern regions of their native habitat.

The broad diversity of these characteristics within *B. versicolor* explains why the *B. versicolor* described by Lagerheim as light brick-red, with smooth branches and leaf blades, bears little similarity to a *Brugmansia* discovered in 1918. In 1921 W. E. Safford described it as a furry, pink-flowered Angel's Trumpet. Nowadays there is no problem in classifying this type of *B. versicolor* as an independent species under the name *Datura mollis*. Unfortunately this name was used incorrectly for all kinds of Angel's Trumpets. The original plant described by Safford as *Datura mollis* was definitely a furry, pink-flowered *B. versicolor* (see page 88).

In spite of wide possibilities of variation in some characteristics, *B. versicolor* is easy to recognize. Its flower corollas are the largest of all the species of *Brugmansia*; they reach a length of 12–20 in (30–50 cm). The basal part of the corolla narrows to a thin, long tube and is always clearly visible. The narrowed part can be up to half of the total length of the flower. It becomes trumpet-shaped, then widens out into large frills on the flower edge and ends in curved peaks that are 1–2½ in (3–6 cm) long.

The bud of a *B. versicolor* is green to greenish yellow. As it opens it turns first white then takes on its final color (*versicolor* = various colors) that, depending on the variety, can be apricot or peach, pink or white.

B. versicolor has a particularly strong scent in the evening, but both the length of its flowers and

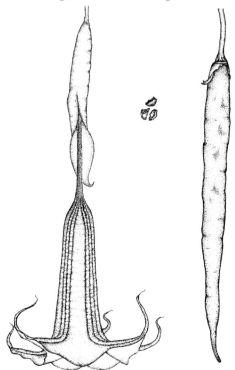

Brugmansia versicolor: flower, seeds and fruit.

Brugmansia versicolor

their drooping position definitely preclude pollination by night moths. Various smaller species of insects are often found within the long flower corollas. Presumably these are attracted by the scent, and land in the corolla where they feed on the pollen. When the insects try to leave the flowers, they have difficulty finding the flower opening as it points downwards. Whether the pollinations, which occur spontaneously in cultivation, can be explained by the resultant, often hectic attempts to fly out is probable, but remains to be proven.

B. versicolor flowers in bursts. In this species the individual growth phases are very distinct. In no other species of *Brugmansia* do so many flowers bloom at the same time. During a flowering phase *B. versicolor* is one mass of flowers. This impressive flowering period can last between two to four weeks. It is followed by a growth phase of one to two months during which time this species

of Angel's Trumpet has no flowers at all though new flower buds continue to form. Once each has reached a certain size it stops growing and waits until sufficient buds have formed for the next flowering phase. All the buds then enter the final development stage together, open at the same time and begin a new flowering phase. During the summer, the plant will have one to three of these flowering phases, depending on the temperature and light conditions and, naturally, on the nutritional condition of the plant.

The calyx is relatively short compared to the overall length of the flower. It is slit on one side, shiny or lightly furry and wraps loosely around the thin flower tube. After pollination it usually falls off but can cover the uppermost part of the fruit as a dry skin. The fruit, which are 10–18 in

(26–45 cm) long, are smooth and thin. In their native habitat they dry and weather while still on the tree before they release the seeds. The seeds (¹/₄ in [8 mm] long) are spread by wind and water like almost all the *Brugmansia*.

In the wild, *B. versicolor* grows into a bush or small tree and reaches an average height of 10¹/₂–17¹/₂ ft (3–5 m). In cultivation, this *Brugmansia* grows well as a standard. This is the perfect form for displaying its long perpendicular flowers at their abundant best.

The leaves of *B. versicolor* are elongated to elliptical in shape with a whole rim. They are smooth or lightly furry.

As has been described, one of the characteristic traits of all varieties of *B. versicolor* is the calyx, which is relatively short compared to the overall length of the flowers. This allows a large portion of the very narrow upper part of the flower section to be visible. Nowadays in cultivation, there are more and more examples of *B. versicolor* with long calyxes that totally cover the narrowed part of the corolla tube. With such examples that differ from the norm in an individual trait, such as a long calyx, you should always consider the possibility that it is a hybrid.

Brugmansia vulcanicola (A. S. Barcley) R. E. Schultes

A. S. Barcley first used the name *Datura vulcanicola* in 1959 to describe a plant whose flowers reminded him of a *Brugmansia sanguinea*. This may have been the reason why some authors tried to classify it as a sub-species of this species. In 1977 R. E. Schultes classified it as an independent species, *B. vulcanicola* within the genus *Brugmansia*.

Opposite page: *Brugmansia versicolor* hybrid f. *plena* 'Herrenhäuser Gärten' with dark orange flowers, description page 90.

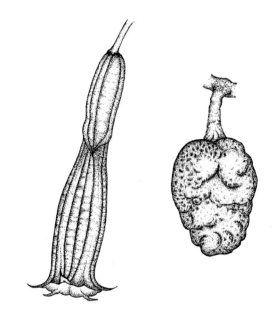

Brugmansia vulcanicola: flower and fruit.

B. vulcanicola is probably the rarest of all the Angel's Trumpets. Even in its native habitat in South America it is known to grow in only a few places and only a few isolated examples grow in each. The most well-known site is the slope of Puracé volcano in southern Colombia (*vulcanica* = growing in volcanic soil), where the plants grow at altitudes of 9800–11,550 ft (2800–3300 m). Until now, *B. vulcanicola* has hardly ever been grown in cultivation.

In 1994, a few seeds of *B. vulcanicola* were successfully gathered from their native habitat in Colombia. They were taken to the Herrenhäuser Gardens, Germany, where they germinated well. They have grown into splendid small trees about 7 ft (2 m) high and are covered in magnificent flowers. Thus the collection of *Brugmansia* at Herrenhäuser Gardens now includes a stock of plants of this genetically different species. There is reason to hope that over the next few years we will be able to harvest sufficient fruit with fertile seeds to enable this very interesting plant to be widely distributed among the various collectors of Angel's Trumpets.

Yellow-flowering example of *Brugmansia vulcanicola*.

all the species of *Brugmansia*. At its widest point the diameter of the corolla tube is 1 in (3 cm) — barely the size of a finger. The *B. vulcanicola* flower has the smallest diameter of all. This dainty Angel's Trumpet has other typical characteristics: its flower veins are only slightly prominent and its flower edge is barely rolled. In spite of this, its flower corolla is as firm in consistency as that of *B. sanguinea*, thanks to a corolla wall that is less than $1/32$ in (1 mm) thick. This guarantees the flower a comparatively long life of five to eight days.

Like *B. sanguinea*, *B. vulcanicola* has a multi-colored form. The color sequence of *B. sanguinea* is a green base, then a yellow middle, and red at the mouth. In *B. vulcanicola* the sequence is green at the base, usually covered by the calyx, then red in the middle, becoming more and more yellow towards the end of the corolla, and finally turning into a shining pure yellow at the mouth. *B. vulcanicola* also has single-colored red and yellow forms where the green base is completely covered by the calyx. A pastel pink-flowered form exists with light pink-colored veins, but this is very rare and only two bushes have been found in the vicinity of La Cocha Lake in Colombia. The dark violet-colored calyx of this plant is particularly unusual.

In comparison to *B. sanguinea*, the gleaming calyx of *B. vulcanicola* wraps tightly around the corolla tube that splits one to three times at the mouth. These peaks often split again into smaller "teeth" of various lengths. In this species of *Brugmansia*, the calyx usually falls off while the fruit is developing.

The fruit of *B. vulcanicola* are more oval-shaped and over 5 in (12 cm) long. They have a wrinkled, warty surface. Their stalk is woody and sticks to the branch. These branches have been described as fibrous and very hard, but not brittle, as in other species of *Brugmansia*. *B. vulcanicola* grows into a bush or small tree up to a height of 14 ft (4 m).

The flowers of *B. vulcanicola* are similar to those of *B. sanguinea*. Both their corollas are tube-shaped and about the same length (6–8$1/2$ in [15–22 cm]). The peaks of *B. vulcanicola* are only $1/16$–$1/2$ in (0.3–1.5 cm) long and are the shortest of

The leaves of this Angel's Trumpet are egg-shaped with deep, rounded indentations on the rim. They have very few hairs and are very shiny. They are very small and in mature plants they are only between 3½–4 in (8–10 cm) long. They provide an excellent foil to the flowers that are very dainty.

The hybrids of *B. vulcanicola* are also very interesting. As well as the single-colored forms in yellow, pink or red, a cross between *B. sanguinea* and *B. vulcanicola* produces the color sequence of a green base, a yellow middle and a red mouth. The

Yellow- and red-flowering example of *Brugmansia vulcanicola.*

calyx shape is typically *B. sanguinea* and the dainty shape of the flower points to *B. vulcanicola*.

Unfortunately, *B. vulcanicola* is not easy to cultivate, as it is particularly susceptible to moisture in the planting mix. For this reason there are not many examples of this rare *Brugmansia* and its existence is endangered. It is to be hoped that this interesting species of plant can be retained by horticultural measures.

Hybrid Angel's Trumpets

Brugmansia x *candida* Persoon *(B. aurea* x
    B. versicolor)
Brugmansia x *flava* Herklotz ex Preissel
    (B. arborea x *B. sanguinea)*
Brugmansia aurea x *B. suaveolens*
Brugmansia insignis x *B. versicolor* and
    Brugmansia suaveolens x *B. versicolor*
Brugmansia aurea x *B. insignis* x *B. suaveolens* x
    B. versicolor

*B*rugmansia are a species of plant that has adapted to a life close to people. Many other plants are pushed to the limit of their existence by people whose activities are usually destructive to nature, but Angel's Trumpets often actually find favorable conditions on disturbed areas such as garbage dumps, unpaved streets or on watercourses. Seedlings are quickly able to outgrow all the competition. Discarded twigs easily form roots and new bushes grow from these. Many a street worker in Ecuador has discovered that cutting off the *Brugmansia* bushes aboveground is not the way to get rid of them, as numerous new bushes grow from the roots. What was intended to be a removal campaign actually results in spreading the stock further.

Natural hybrids are frequently found within the natural distribution area of *Brugmansia*. *B.* x *candida*, *B. suaveolens* x *B. versicolor* and *B. insignis* x *B. suaveolens* are the most prevalent. But *B.* x *flava*, which was widespread in European collections during the last century, probably developed in South America as well.

People have made a considerable contribution to the development of hybrids. It was people, after all, who, by taking these decorative plants into their gardens and cemeteries, ensured that they spread, and thus removed natural geographic barriers and provided the prerequisites for the formation of hybrids.

Whether or not hybrids of *B. aurea* x *B. suaveolens* occur naturally is unfortunately not known. Numerous crossbreeding successes in the past have proven that this combination is possible. The same applies to all multiple hybrids *(B. aurea* x *B. insignis* x *B. suaveolens* x *B. versicolor)*.

Brugmansia x *candida* Persoon

The "Flora Peruviana" published by Ruiz and Pavon in 1799 contained an illustration of a *Brugmansia* that was incorrectly classified as *Datura arborea*. In 1805, C. H. Persoon based his description of *Brugmansia candida* on this illustration and on the description of the plant that was provided with it.

Until 1973, when T. E. Lockwood recognized their hybrid nature *(B.* x *candida)* and carried out experiments to prove it, these plants were considered to be an independent species. In the wild, *B.* x *candida* grows only on the western and

eastern slopes of the Ecuadorean Andes at heights of 3500–5250 ft (1000–1500 m). People introduced and colonized both parent plants, *B. aurea* and *B. versicolor*. What were apparently spontaneous hybridizations between the two species produced plants that fit exactly the description given by Persoon — a plant that he called *B. candida*. The experiments carried out in cultivation between *B. aurea* and *B. versicolor* finally confirmed the hybrid nature of *B. x candida*.

B. x *candida* grows and flowers in places up to 7000 ft (2000 m) high. It is very decorative and is tolerant of the most diverse environmental conditions. For these reasons, these Angel's Trumpets were spread far and wide some time ago. Today, they are found in northern Chile, in Peru,

This *Brugmansia* x *candida* developed from the crossing of *B. versicolor* x *B. aurea*.

Ecuador, and Colombia, in Mexico and on the Caribbean Islands. *B.* x *candida* was one of the first *Brugmansia* to be taken to Africa and Europe and is now widely cultivated in those places.

In flower shape, size and color, this Angel's Trumpet fills a position in the middle between *B. aurea* and *B. versicolor*. Its strongly fragrant flowers range from 9–13 in (23–33 cm) in length. In contrast to those of *B. versicolor,* they have only a slight narrowing of the corolla tube outside the calyx. Their flower edge opens out wide. It is puffed up and ends in peaks 1–2½ in (2–6 cm) long that curve backwards. The flower colors are

49

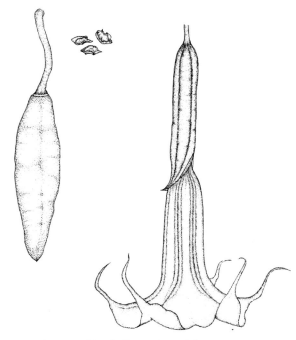

Brugmansia x candida: fruit, seeds and flower.

white (*candida* = snow white), yellow to apricot and occasionally pink. They are predominantly pendulous.

B. x candida flowers in bursts. The difference between the various growth phases is not as distinct as in *B. versicolor*. These Angel's Trumpets are never completely without flowers. Under suitable cultivation conditions and in warmer climates, i.e. sufficient light with good nutrition and minimal temperatures between 53°–64°F (12°–18°C), most of the *B. x candida* varieties also flower during the winter months. Together with the various *B. suaveolens* varieties, they are the most prolific flowerers and the most reliable of all the *Brugmansia*. Unfavorable weather conditions — except cold — do not discourage it from flowering.

The calyx of *B. x candida* is slit on one side and is thus similar to that of *B. versicolor*. The apex of the calyx on the opposite side of the slit either stands up like a horn or is split further. Usually the surface of the calyx wraps loosely around the narrowed part of the flower tube. Sometimes it looks slightly puffed up. Its surface is shiny and lightly furry. After successful pollination its remains stay stuck to the fruit as it develops.

The fruit are covered in velvety hairs but it is not possible to give definitive data on their shape or length as they can be found in every imaginable variation between the elongated fruit of *B. versicolor* and the egg-shaped ones of *B. aurea*. Like the fruit of *B. aurea*, they weather while still on the tree until the destruction of the outer skin releases the seeds. The leaves, which are covered in light hairs, are oval to elliptical in shape. Their rims are either dentated or whole.

One peculiarity noticed first on *B. x candida* is the appearance of double-flowering types. Their flower corollas consist of at least two corollas, one lying within the other. The inner one is often tightly folded, incompletely formed and can be split to the base on one side. The creamy white-flowered *plena* that is widely cultivated is one example of this double-flowering type. Its flowers are about 10 in (25 cm) long and appear puffed up in their middle because of the double corolla.

As *B. x candida* is a hybrid form between *B. aurea* and *B. versicolor*, Persoon's description of the original plant is only applicable as a classification tool to one of the varieties of *B. x candida*. Every imaginable variation is possible between the two parent plants. Further problems in classification are created by the fact that *B. x candida* lends itself particularly easily to being recrossed with *B. aurea* and *B. versicolor*. This produces plants that differ only minimally from the pure parent plant. Quite often this variation falls within the natural limits of variation of the wild species. An exact classification of such a plant is no longer possible. As examples we should mention the Indian forms of *B. aurea* that were listed on page 33, i.e. 'Biangan', 'Quinde' or 'Ocre', which display typical characteristics of both *B. x candida* and *B. aurea* and therefore are found in cultivation under both classifications.

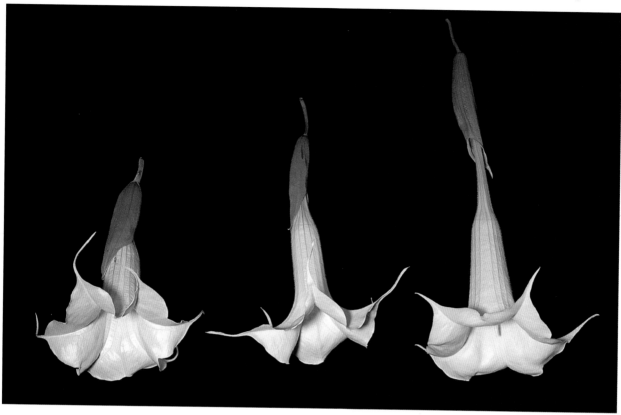

The F1 generation (middle of picture) of the crossbreeding of *Brugmansia aurea* (left) and *B. versicolor* (right) has been given the formula *B. x candida*. Usually it takes an intermediary position and has by comparison a unique appearance.

Brugmansia x *flava*
Herklotz ex Preissel

The Angel's Trumpet known today under the name *B. x flava* was one of the first *Brugmansia* cultivated in European gardens. Unfortunately, it is not known who originally discovered or cultivated it.

For some time this was the only plant to be called *Brugmansia* commercially and the name "Angel's Trumpet" or "*Datura*" was sufficient to distinguish it from other plants. The increasing popularity of Angel's Trumpets with gardening enthusiasts has led to a wider distribution of the most diverse species of *Brugmansia* and thus to the necessity to label them all. In the Herrenhäuser Gardens, in the 1970s, this plant was classified by A. Herklotz as *B. x flava* for the first time, to explain its hybrid nature. A. Herklotz died prematurely and did not publish the collective name *B. x flava* again. In order for the name to retain validity and comply with the rules of botanical nomenclature, we published it in the German edition of this book.

Unlike almost all other Angel's Trumpets, *B. x flava* has characteristics that are very typical of a species and point clearly to its two parents. Only the style of *B. arborea* is furry. The styles of *B. x flava* are lightly furry. Only the corolla of *B. sanguinea* is tube-shaped. The corolla of *B. x flava* is distinctly tube-shaped. The flowers are 8–12 in (21–30 cm) long and have hardly any scent. They are always positioned at an angle on the branch. The narrowed part of the corolla is completely covered by the calyx, which is slit on one side. The attached tube-shaped section ends in peaks

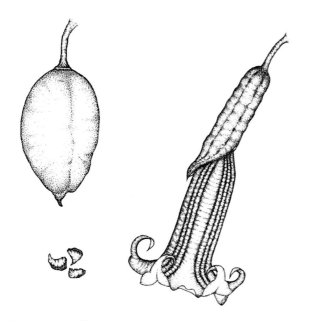

Brugmansia x *flava*: fruit, seeds and flower.

that are 1–1½ in (2–4 cm) long and curve backwards.

The yellowish green flower veins, which are furry, are very prominent, as they are on *B. sanguinea*. This considerably increases the stability of the corollas and explains why the individual flowers last for a relatively long time, which compensates somewhat for the plant's tendency to produce fewer flowers during the hot summer months. *B. sanguinea* shows a marked tendency to reduce flower production when temperatures are high and bequeathed this trait to *B.* x *flava*. *B.* x *flava* flowers with great dependability at the beginning and at the end of each summer vegetation period and will also flower during the summer if it is cooler.

Initially, its flowers were colored exclusively in shades of yellow, as the name (*flava* = yellow) indicates. More recently, we have been successful in transferring other colors from the parent species, such as white, pink, orange and red. Plants have also been developed with flowers of an intense violet-blue. This color was totally unknown in varieties of Angel's Trumpets. Like its parent *B. sanguinea*, *B.* x *flava* will have both single colors and combinations of colors (green at the base, yellow in the middle, red at the mouth).

Nowadays, it is impossible to say with certainty whether similar plants have existed in the past. As early as 1921, W. E. Safford described a red-flowered plant as *Datura rubella* (see page 62), even though the flowers were much smaller (5–5½ in [13–14 cm]). Because of major differences in the sizes of flower, leaf and fruit and the different proportions of calyx to corolla between *B.* x *flava* and *Datura rubella*, it does not seem logical to consider both examples as the same type of plant.

The calyx of *B.* x *flava* is velvety, furry and deeply slit on one side. The peak opposite the slit can stand up like a horn or be split into smaller "teeth". Because of the prominent veins, the calyx often gives the impression of being slightly puffed up. The calyx never wraps around the flower corolla as tightly as it does in *B. arborea*. Compared to the overall length of the flower, the length of the calyx in *B.* x *flava* is always noticeably shorter than in *B. arborea*.

The leaves are egg- to lance-shaped and are also covered in velvety fur. The edges of the leaves are clearly dentated.

The elongated fruit are light green to yellowish in color. They are about 4–4½ in (9–11 cm) long and have a diameter of over 2 in (5 cm). Only the fruits of *B. sanguinea* and *B. vulcanicola* are known to need the same relatively long time span of eight to nine months for the seeds to ripen. The seeds are flattened and ½ in (14 mm) long.

B. x *flava* also grows in a similar way to *B. sanguinea*. The branches start to fork very early on and form a bush with dense foliage that often goes right down to the ground. This makes the plants look decorative even without flowers. As cuttings of *B.* x *flava* flower well while still small plants, they are particularly suited for places with little space.

Tricolored example of *Brugmansia* x *flava*. Above left: Tuberous thickening on the roots of *Brugmansia* x *flava*.

Brugmansia x *flava* between its parent species *B. sanguinea* (on the left) and *B. arborea* (on the right).

Peculiar tuberous formations are frequently found in the root area of *B.* x *flava*. Similar tubers are occasionally found on *B. sanguinea*, but they are extremely rare. None has been found on *B. arborea*. The tuberous thickenings develop not only on seedlings but also on plants grown from cuttings. This tends to restrict root formation with the result that it takes a long time before they can form a dense root system. Apparently, the tuberous thickenings are like roots and have the ability to take up water and nutrients directly from the substrate.

To date there has been no explanation of the morphological structure of the tuberous shapes, why they appear in *B.* x *flava* hybrids and what function they perform for the plant. Possibly, they are survival and propagation organs similar to those of *Datura inoxia* or *D. wrightii*. This explanation is supported by the fact that sprouts regularly develop on them.

On the other hand, the striking tuberous shapes are not necessary for shoots to form from the soil. Both *B.* x *flava* and *B. sanguinea* have the ability to form new vegetation points on their roots. This characteristic is rare. It means that even when the plants have been totally cleared away, new shoots can develop from the roots that have remained in the ground.

Hybrids from *Brugmansia aurea* x *B. suaveolens*

Hybrids of *B. aurea* x *B. suaveolens* are primarily known from being cultivated in gardens. There are no indications that these extremely decorative Angel's Trumpets spread naturally in the South American region.

In 1949 P. C. Joshi was the first to prove that this cross could be carried out successfully. He was only able to produce this hybrid form when he used *B. suaveolens* as the mother plant.

The flowers of the hybrids of *B. aurea* x *B. suaveolens* are strikingly similar to those of *B. suaveolens*. As in these, the corolla is funnel-shaped. The flowers, which are mainly white, vary between 8¹/₂–14¹/₂ in (22–36 cm) in length. The anthers are glued to some extent. Taking all these factors into consideration, it is easy to understand why many of these hybrid plants are classified as *B. suaveolens*.

Yet, it is not particularly difficult to identify a hybrid of *B. aurea* x *B. suaveolens*. These plants almost always have long peaks of 1–3 in (2–8 cm) in length which are often twisted in spirals. Only a short part of the tube-shaped, narrowed part of the corolla is visible, if at all, outside the calyx. The consistency of the corolla wall is clearly more stable than that of *B. suaveolens*, which means that the individual flowers last a long time.

After successful pollination, the calyx usually falls off. Occasionally, its dried remains stay wrapped around the elongated oval fruit.

The leaves of many *B. aurea* x *B. suaveolens* hybrids look like those of *B. aurea*. If they are well fertilized and have sufficient water in summer they will also grow up to 28 in (70 cm) in length.

This hybrid form is a highly recommended Angel's Trumpet because of its many excellent qualities. It flowers well and continuously both during the summer and during the winter months, even when the conditions for its growth cannot be considered to be optimal. It is a rampant grower. The very large leaves often obscure the flowers and need to be broken off.

Cuttings of *B. aurea* x *B. suaveolens* taken from the flowering region will flower while still small plants of about 20 in (50 cm) tall — that is, three to four months after they have rooted. The young plants grow fast and soon develop into imposing bushes with a corresponding need for space. To be displayed at their decorative best, they need to be grown as individual plants with plenty of space around them.

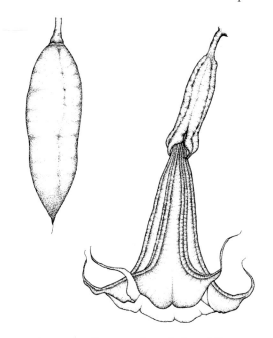

Brugmansia aurea x *B. suaveolens*: fruit and flower.

Hybrids from *Brugmansia insignis* x *B. versicolor* and *Brugmansia suaveolens* x *B. versicolor*

At first glance, because the flowers of the hybrids of *B. versicolor* and *B. insignis* or *B. suaveolens* are usually pendulous, they often look very like the wild species *B. versicolor*. Consequently, they

Hybrids of *Brugmansia aurea* x *B. suaveolens* usually have nodding flowers with long peaks. The flower wall is frequently wavy at right angles to the flower veins.

are often confused. Most of the narrowed part of the corolla tube outside the calyx is also clearly visible. On closer examination it is apparent that the flower corolla is more of a mixture of trum-

pet- and funnel-shaped. Hybrids with *B. suaveolens* often have distinctive short peaks on the petals that are not rolled back. *B. insignis*, on the other hand, bequeaths rather longer petal peaks that are frequently bent forwards. The calyx of these hybrids is usually deeply slit on one side and the peak opposite the slit is divided into further small teeth.

Brugmansia hybrid 'Pride of Hannover'

The anthers of many of these hybrid forms are still slightly glued. This is a sure indicator that *B. suaveolens* or *B. insignis* is a participant in this hybrid. Unfortunately, types with unglued anthers also occur.

These hybrids may not be easy to classify, but they are easy to cultivate. Most of these plants flower throughout the whole summer in continually recurring bursts of flowers, even when the weather conditions are unfavorable. As regards frequency of flowering, this plant type is thus a visible improvement on the wild species *B. versicolor*. An example of a hybrid between *B. suaveolens* with *B. versicolor* is the beautiful variety 'Rosa Glockenfontäne'. It originates in Colombia and has flowers that are about 15³/₄ in (40 cm) long. The variety 'Pride of Hannover' was the result of a hybrid of *B. insignis* with *B. versicolor*. Its flowers are often 17³/₄ in (45 cm) long and have a diameter of 8 in (20 cm).

Hybrids from *Brugmansia aurea* x *B. insignis* x *B. suaveolens* x *B. versicolor*

One of the most striking characteristics of many hybrids is that they are prepared to accept the pollen of Angel's Trumpets that are compatible and therefore set fruit easily. They are thus ideally suited for breeding new varieties. Growers are always tempted by the possibility of combining a larger number of characteristics specific to a species. It was not long before the first hybrids were developed that bore the inherited characteristics of up to four different species. Here is an example for clarification: If *B. x candida* (a hybrid of *B. aurea* x *B. versicolor*) is crossed with a hybrid from *B. insignis* x *B. suaveolens*, then the result is a multihybrid that will have inherited the characteristics of four different species.

Many of these hybrids may be dreamily beautiful but they are very difficult, if not impossible, to classify exactly. The classification keys on pages 26–27 are unfortunately no use either. The combination of the chararacteristics of the different species simply produces too many different shapes. The *Brugmansia* enthusiast can therefore enjoy their unclassifiable Angel's Trumpet with a clear conscience. Like the *Brugmansia* hybrid 'Charles Grimaldi' it may have the flower length of a *B. versicolor*, the flower corolla shape of a *B. suaveolens*, the petal tip length of a *B. aurea* and petal tips that bend fowards slightly like those of a *B. insignis*.

Right: *Brugmansia suaveolens* x *B. versicolor*: fruit and flower.

How the flower corolla changes from trumpet- to funnel-shaped is best seen by a direct comparison. The picture shows a *Brugmansia versicolor* with trumpet-shaped flowers into which a flower of the hybrid *B. insignis* x *B. versicolor* (which shows a transition stage to funnel-shaped) was suspended.

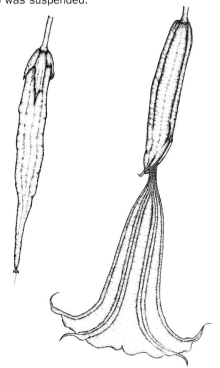

Are there other species?

Many *Brugmansia* growers may have looked in vain for their Angel's Trumpet in the previous chapters. Perhaps it has a label with the description *Brugmansia mollis*, *B. rosei* or *B. dolichocarpa*. What is hidden behind these names?

To get a better understanding of the system of botanical nomenclature, we have to digress briefly and discuss how a species is named. There are four major steps:

1. Choice of a Latin name for the plant.
2. Description of their traits that will identify the species of plant.
3. Deposit of a typical plant (flower, leaf, fruit, etc.) in a preserved form in a public herbarium with exact data on where it was found and its geographical distribution.
4. Publication of all data (name, Latin diagnosis, place where deposited, etc.) in a scientific journal or a book.

Where corrections are made later, the name of the person who made the first classification is put in brackets in front of the author who made the correction.

Example: In 1753 Linnaeus classified a plant as *Datura arborea*. Its exact classification is therefore *D. arborea* Linnaeus. In 1895 Lagerheim classified it into the genus *Brugmansia*. Since then the correct classification has been *B. arborea* (Linnaeus) Lagerheim.

The date of the first publication of the valid name is decisive. Should the same plant type be described at a later date under another name out of ignorance or by ignoring the initial publication, then the later name is always invalid. It becomes a synonym of the correct name. Example: *B. bicolor* is a synonym for *B. sanguinea*, as this plant was first classified as *B. sanguinea* five years previously.

All those genera whose species, like the *Brugmansia*, display a wide variation of characteristics within a species are highly susceptible to double namings. Who can be absolutely certain where the variations within a species stops and a new species begins? This is how the names *B. mollis* and *B. rosei* developed. Both are classifications of plants that today fall within the permitted limits of a species that had been classified previously.

Where possible, the original description (see 4 above) of the names below will be quoted in an abridged version. Nowadays, these classifications often apply to totally different plants and have nothing else more in common with the plant that was originally classified. The samples of some *Brugmansia*, classified in the 19th century, have been lost. This presents a totally different set of problems. Because the original descriptions were often incomplete, it is not possible to clearly identify many of these plants. One example is *B. dolichocarpa*. This is why it is preferable not

Opposite page: In their natural habitat, Angel's Trumpets like these *Brugmansia sanguinea* at La Bonita, Ecuador, frequently grow on the edge of areas that are used for agriculture. (Photo: A. Holguin.)

to use these names for plants that are currently available.

Datura affinis Safford, 1921
Invalid classification for *Brugmansia aurea*.

In 1895 Lagerheim published his theory that the white-flowering *B. aurea* was in fact the *B. arborea* that had been classified in 1753. Safford took note of this earlier mistake and reclassified the white-flowering *B. aurea* as *Datura affinis* (*affinis* = similar, related) because of its similarity to the yellow-flowering *B. aurea*.

Brugmansia bicolor Persoon, 1805
Invalid classification of *Brugmansia sanguinea*.

In 1799 Ruíz and Pavon were the first to classify this species under the name *Datura sanguinea*.

Datura chlorantha flore pleno Hooker, 1859
Original description
Growth form: like a tree
Leaf: lance- to egg-shaped (similar to the leaf of *B. arborea*), shining
Flower: pendulous, yellow, double (double corolla)
Peaks: curved backwards
Calyx: dentated five times.

In 1845 Hooker discovered his *D. chlorantha* in a garden in England. He described it as tree-like and therefore classified it into the *Brugmansia* section.

This yellow double-flowered Angel's Trumpet was probably a cultivated form of *B.* x *candida*. Unfortunately, there is no information available on whether this plant is still being cultivated and, if so, to what extent.

Problems arose for the first time, in 1894, when a yellow double-flowered *D. metel* was also classified under the name *D. chlorantha*. The combination of the correct classification made in 1859 and the plant classified in 1894 has caused some confusion.

Datura cornigera Hooker, 1846
Invalid classification of *Brugmansia arborea*.

The illustration on which the first classification of *B. arborea* was based in 1753 shows an extremely rare variant of the calyx with split peaks. In 1846, when Hooker classified the normal plant with calyx peaks standing up like a horn, he believed he was classifying a new species and gave it the name *D. cornigera* (*corniger* = bearing a horn).

Brugmansia dolichocarpa Lagerheim, 1895
Original description
Growth form: like a bush or a tree
Leaf: lance- to egg-shaped, not furry
Flower: white, 13–14 in (34–35 cm) long, upper part of the corolla narrowed to a tube, veins furry
Flower edge: widened
Peak: 1$\frac{1}{2}$–2 in (3.5–5 cm) long, part lying between peaks is rounded
Calyx: 4$\frac{1}{2}$–5 in (11–13 cm) long, dentated two to five times, smooth
Fruit: furry, cylindrical to spindle-shaped, 11$\frac{1}{2}$–12$\frac{1}{2}$ in (29–31 cm)
Seeds: flattened, color: brownish yellow

Lagerheim wrote of his *B. dolichocarpa* that it was closely related to *B. suaveolens* and *B. versicolor*. Its long fruit, shaped like cotton reels (*dolichocarpa* = with long fruit), its free-standing anthers, long peaks and seeds were all typical characteristics.

We assume that *B. dolichocarpa* is a hybrid of *B. versicolor*. As most of the hybrids from *B. suaveolens* x *B. versicolor* have short peaks, it could possibly be a recrossing with *B. versicolor*. We cannot identify *B. dolichocarpa* more specifically because, in addition to the description, we have only a photograph of the material in the herbarium on which the original classification was based. The sample itself was destroyed in Berlin during World War II.

Datura frutescens Hort. Siebert & Voss, 1895
Invalid name for *Brugmansia arborea*.

Datura gardneri Hooker, 1846
Invalid name for *Brugmansia suaveolens*.

In 1809 Willdenow was the first to describe this species under the name *Datura suaveolens*.

Datura knightii Siebert & Voss, 1895
Invalid name for *Brugmansia arborea*.

Brugmansia longifolia Lagerheim, 1895
Original description
Growth form: Bush, 6¹/₂–7 ft (2–3 m) high
Leaf: long, with edges curved like coves
Flower: white, 11–12 in (27–30 cm) long, upper part of the corolla narrowed to a tube
Flower edge: curved slightly outwards
Peaks: 1¹/₂ in (4 cm) long, curved inwards
Calyx: 4–5 in (10–12 cm) long, dentated two to five times
Fruit: no sign of fruit

Lagerheim made particular note of the long, narrow leaves with their undulated indentations (*longifolius* = long-leafed).

Unfortunately, there is no exact data available on length. Most likely, the leaves of *B. longifolia* are similar to those of either *B. aurea* hybrid 'Culebra' or *B. insignis*.

The distinctive funnel shape of the flower corolla and the very narrowed base part of the corolla tube outside the calyx, which can be seen on the photographs of the original sample, make the latter more likely. Lagerheim's note about the total lack of fruit is important. This characteristic usually occurs only on *B. insignis* that is growing in the wild.

Unfortunately, we can only guess that the description of *B. longifolia* fitted a type that was similar to *B. insignis*. As with *B. dolichocarpa*, the material in the herbarium, which was used for classification, was destroyed during the war.

Brugmansia lutea Hort. ex Gard. Chron. 1888
Invalid name for *B. sanguinea*.

Datura mollis Safford, 1921
Invalid name for *B. versicolor*.
Original description
Growth form: bush or small tree
Leaf: furry, oval and elongated, partly dentated, 8¹/₂ in long x 4 in wide (22 x 10.5 cm)
Flower: 10–10¹/₂ in (25–27 cm) long, light pink upper half of the corolla very narrow, widens out to the edge, veins furry
Peaks: 2¹/₂–3 in (6–7 cm) long, curved
Calyx: slit on one side, approximately 8 in (19–20 cm) long, furry.

In 1921 Safford, using material in the herbarium, described a plant collected by J. N. Rose. This example was classified as *Datura mollis* and was found in the southern section of the natural habitat of *Brugmansia versicolor* (region around Portovelo, Ecuador).

Lockwood's data described the main stock of this species of plant as being furry and having relatively small flowers (see page 42). Therefore the description of *D. mollis* probably refers to an example of *B. versicolor* that is furry and has pink flowers.

Datura pittieri Safford, 1921
Invalid name for *Brugmansia aurea*.
Original description
Flower: 7 in (18 cm) long, trumpet-shaped (no details on color)
Peaks: over 1¹/₂ in (4 cm) in length, curved
Calyx: slit on one side, peaks split again
Fruit: 5 in (13 cm) long, 2 in (5.5 cm) wide, elongated to egg-shaped

In Safford's opinion the different examples of *B. aurea* (variations in flower color and number of dentations in the calyx) were different species. According to current classification methods, his description of *D. pittori* fits *B. aurea*.

Datura rosei Safford, 1921

Invalid name for *B. sanguinea*.

Original description

Leaf: very furry, dentated

Flower: tube-shaped, 6–7 in (15.5–18.5 cm) long, furry, orange or yellow, green veins

Peaks: ¹/₂ in (1–1.5 cm)

Calyx: dentated two to five times, furry

Fruit: egg-shaped, furry, 2¹/₂ in (7 cm) long, 1¹/₂ in (4.5 cm) wide, covered with dried residue of calyx.

Safford obtained the plant material for this initial description from J. N. Rose, after whom the species was named *rosei* and who pointed out the striking similarity between *D. rosei* and *B. sanguinea*. According to current methods used for classification, the ways it differed from the example of *B. sanguinea* described in 1799, which had mainly red flowers, are all within the natural variation range of this species.

Datura rubella Safford, 1921

Original description

Growth form: 6¹/₂–10 ft (2.5–3 m) high bushes

Leaf: furry, oval to lance-like in shape

Flower: red, 5–5¹/₂ in (13–14 cm) long, does not open very wide, veins furry

Peaks: ¹/₂ in (1.5 cm) long

Calyx: furry, 4 in (10 cm) long, slit on one side, the opposing peak standing up

Fruit: oval- to lemon-shaped, 2¹/₂ in (7 cm) long, 2 in (5 cm) wide.

If you ignore the color of the flowers of this plant that was classified exclusively from material in the herbarium, then you would think you were looking at a *B. arborea*. This explains why, in 1973, Lockwood assumed it was a hybridization between *B. arborea* and a red *B. sanguinea*. The cross between *B. arborea* and a yellow *B. sanguinea* (*B.* x *flava*, see page 85), which is nowadays very common, is very different as regards the size of its flowers and fruit. The size ratio of length of calyx to length of flower is also important. The calyx length of *B.* x *flava* is 4 in (11 cm), while the flowers measure about 8 in (21 cm). *D. rubella* also has a calyx of 4 in (11 cm), but its flowers are only 5–5¹/₂ in (13–14 cm) long.

There is uncertainty over the exact color of the flower of this plant described as *D. rubella* (*rubella* = reddish), as it is very possible the material in the herbarium, on which the classification was based, had changed color. The plant collector J. N. Rose left no information on the color of the flowers he collected as early as 1918.

Datura speciosa Salisbury, 1796

Invalid description for *B. arborea*.

Angel's Trumpets as a container plant

In North American climate zones, except in zone 10, Angel's Trumpets are grown mainly in containers. Although summer temperatures suit them, they would not survive an inland winter outdoors because they are frost-tender plants. In general, they cannot withstand temperatures below freezing, 32°F (0°C). Some important facts need to be borne in mind if they are to develop to their optimum.

Planters

Always choose large, wide containers. This ensures that water and nutrients are supplied at a constant rate. A large amount of soil also improves the stability of these plants that are often covered in foliage and tend to be top-heavy. A fairly deep layer of gravel on the bottom of the container increases the weight of the tub and at the same time reduces the danger of the plant having wet feet, as this can cause even such water-greedy plants as *Brugmansia* to die.

Large planters ensure water and nutrients are supplied at a constant rate.

It is extremely important that water is continually drained from the planter. There should be several openings of sufficient size on the bottom of the tub. Ensure that these do not become blocked by clumps of substrate, otherwise it is very easy for water to accumulate in the tub. If this cannot be monitored and the soil becomes saturated, the roots will rot. How important it is to have good drainage becomes obvious whenever there is a heavy thunderstorm. It can fill a slow-draining container to the rim within a few minutes.

It is a matter of personal choice whether you select a plastic, wood or clay container. These various materials have different characteristics as described briefly below:

Planters made of plastic

All plastic planters are very light. This is a positive property when potting or removing Angel's Trumpets, but, unfortunately makes the tub less stable when it is planted. The remedy is to give extra weight to the bottom of the tub by increasing the layer of gravel.

Plastic planters have smooth walls that are impermeable to water and on which neither chalk nor fertilizer residues can deposit. The smoothness of the walls also stops the fine root hairs from adhering and makes repotting relatively easy.

Planters made of wood

Oak is suitable for building durable planters. On average they will last six to nine years. To help make them last longer, either burn out the inner wall of the tub leaving a thin wood carbon layer, or paint with linseed oil or ship's tar. If buying wooden tubs, ensure that the bottom planks of the container are a sufficient distance from the ground to allow water to drain and prevent the wood from rotting. If necessary, push additional wood underneath the tub to ensure free drainage.

Planters made of clay and terracotta

Clay containers, particularly those with steep sides, are extremely stable because they are heavy. They are, however, difficult to move. A clay tub that is 16 in (40 cm) high with a diameter of 16 in (40 cm) can weigh up to 110 lbs (50 kg) when it is planted. Unfortunately, all clay containers break easily, which considerably increases the difficulty of potting and repotting the Angel's Trumpets grown in them.

Unglazed terracotta containers have very porous walls through which some water continually evaporates. Angel's Trumpets need a great deal of water, and to provide this, *Brugmansia* grown in untreated clay containers must be watered more often and more thoroughly. Also, part of the dissolved nutrients plus deposited plaster from the clay material migrates to the outer wall of the tub with the water and deposits a grayish white, hard covering that is ugly.

Planting mix

Angel's Trumpets require a planting mix that has a high capacity for storing water and nutrients. All-purpose soils and the peat mixes that are sold commercially consist of about 20 percent clay material and 80 percent peat. They are best suited to young plants that need to be repotted more frequently during the first few years.

When potting large Angel's Trumpets, it is recommended that you mix in about one-third

Brugmansia aurea hybrid 'Culebra' in front of a blue-flowered *Solanum rantonnetii*, description pages 33 and 82.

garden soil containing loam. The higher loam proportion improves both the stability of the plant in the tub as well as its storage capacity. Commercial mixtures with bark are highly recommended for growing *Brugmansia*, but these too need to have a third of soil containing loam mixed in.

Important: test water drainage.

Repotting

As a rule, Angel's Trumpets should be repotted every year; at the least, after two years. By this time, these plants, with their enormous appetite for nutrients, will have totally used up the potting mix and filled it with roots.

Repotting should be done in spring when you are moving the plants out of their winter quarters. Once the plants are out of their pots, examine them for rotting parts and remove any parts that have died off and are crumbly. Do not tear apart healthy balls of roots when doing this. It is sufficient to carefully remove any layers of algae or moss from the surface of the substrate.

The new tubs should be bigger. First put a 2–4 in (5–10 cm) layer of drainage material, depending on size of pot and material. If you are using this to give a plastic planter weight, then use coarse gravel. For large, heavy clay pots use pumice or scoria or a similar material that is lighter. Put fresh potting mix on top of the drainage layer and then put the plant in carefully. Fill all the remaining spaces with fresh mix then water the Angel's Trumpet until the water comes out the lower openings in the tub. If after a few minutes there is water still standing on the surface of the potting mix then immediately examine and rework the drainage.

If you are retaining the same container size, then carefully remove 1½–2 in (2–5 cm) of root-bound soil from the outer edge of the old ball of roots. The easiest way is to use a clean, sharp knife. To prevent the cutting surfaces from rotting, powder the damaged root parts with charcoal powder.

Watering

In spring when the plants start to sprout, their need for water also increases, reaching its maximum during the main period of growth in the summer. Depending on the weather and the humidity, the plants will need to be watered mornings and evenings. The ball of roots must be soaked thoroughly until water flows out of the drainage holes in the bottom of the tub. Try to adjust the amount of water to what the mix can absorb. Excessive amounts will flush out nutrients as well.

On sunny days or when it is very windy, *Brugmansia* need water much more than they do during a period of rain. Occasionally, they do have to be watered even when it is raining. The enormous masses of flowers often act like an umbrella and protect the roots so well that hardly a drop of water reaches the potting mix.

If the ball of roots is dry, then the leaves will droop. If they are watered immediately, then the plants recover amazingly quickly with apparently no further damage. If the need for water is ignored, many species of *Brugmansia* will react by shedding their flower buds or the immature fruit.

After longer periods of rain with subsequent intense sunshine, Angel's Trumpets will sometimes have droopy leaves, even though their roots are supplying sufficient moisture. The plants usually adjust to the new weather conditions within a short time by reinforcing the leaves' ability to protect themselves from evaporation. If *Brugmansia* are left to stand continually in full sun during extremely hot weather, then the roots cannot supply enough water to the leaves during the day.

Frequent sprinkling is beneficial not only to plants standing in full sun but to all Angel's Trumpets in general. The thorough cleansing of dust and dirt particles from the leaves improves assimilation and water uptake through the splits in the leaves. Increasing the humidity around the plant, even if only briefly, reduces evaporation. As the roots are continuing to supply water, this method is particularly effective for revitalizing "sluggish" plants. Frequent sprinkling of the whole plant also disturbs various pests, such as leaf bugs, aphids, and spider mites; this is another positive side effect.

Angel's Trumpets need a great deal of water.

Towards the end of the vegetation period, temperatures become cooler and *Brugmansia*'s need for water is consequently reduced. Water supply should be adapted to the reduced growth of the plants; however, never let the root balls dry out completely.

Site

Note the following points when choosing a suitable site for Angel's Trumpets:

The location should receive plenty of light but be out of direct sunlight during the heat of the day. Plants with a large leaf surface, like so many species of *Brugmansia*, are stimulated by too much direct sunlight and evaporation can be excessive. Even a healthy, highly efficient root system is not able to take up sufficient water to

The optimum location receives plenty of light and is protected from the wind.

balance out this high loss of moisture. In spite of sufficient watering, these plants look "listless" and their growth is visibly poorer compared to those that are standing in light shade.

The location should be protected from wind. The leaves of many *Brugmansia*, such as *B. aurea*, *B. suaveolens* or *B.* x *candida*, offer the wind too large a target area. Even occasional gusts of wind will tear and tousle them and spoil their picture-book beauty. Wind will also damage the flower corollas of species with thin-walled flowers, such as *B. suaveolens*, *B. versicolor* and *B. insignis*. *B. arborea*, its hybrids (*B.* x *flava*), and *B. vulcanicola* have proved to be the least affected by wind.

Fertilization

Angel's Trumpets need regular, large quantities of fertilizer if they are to blossom to their full capacity. When choosing the fertilizer, care should be taken to buy only products where the packaging gives details of the contents. It is recommended that water-soluble fertilizing salts contain around 15 percent nitrogen (N), 5–10 percent phosphate (P_2O_5) and 10–15 percent potassium oxide (K_2O). Mineral liquid fertilizers should have 12 percent nitrogen, about 4 percent phosphate and 7–10 percent potassium oxide.

The recommended concentration of water-soluble salts for *Brugmansia* is 1 teaspoon (4–5 g) nutrient salts per 1½ pints (1 liter) of water and 1 teaspoon (4–5 mL) per 1½ pints (1 liter) of water for mineral liquid fertilizers. These are certainly very high dosages of fertilizer, but they make sense when you actually see how much the plant grows during a summer period.

During the summer vegetation period, fertilize once or twice a week. At these times, when watering the plants, just dissolve the fertilizer into the usual amount of water. Angel's Trumpets that are not given enough fertilizer soon show typical symptoms of a lack of nitrogen: their growth is stunted, they have small leaves that are pale green in color, and the older leaves die and are shed early.

Brugmansia which receive sufficient fertilizer will produce two leaves and then produce a flower. An additional dose of fertilizer will cause them to produce shoots from the vegetation points in the leaf axils. These often develop into truncated shoots with up to five additional flowers. Angel's Trumpets that are heavily fertilized will produce four to five times as many flowers as those that are not.

Brugmansia that are going to over-winter in the cold do not need any fertilizer after the end of August. They should gradually stop growing by fall. When it is warm during the winter, the plants continue to grow though not as fast. A light dose of fertilizer of ¼ teaspoon (1.5 g or 1.5 mL) per 1½ pints (1 liter) of water per week improves flower production in the greenhouse over winter.

Pruning

The most frequent reason for heavy pruning in fall is that space will be restricted where the plants are going to over-winter. Thanks to their great ability to regenerate, most Angel's Trumpets will tolerate even radical pruning measures, almost down to the top of the tub, without suffering lasting damage.

Pruning should, however, be restricted to the flowering part of the plant (see page 21). More radical pruning to the vegetative region will result in a longer period of flowerless growth in the following spring.

All slow-growing Angel's Trumpets, such as *B. aurea* hybrid 'Culebra' or *B. vulcanicola*, should only be given a light trim. If the size of the over-wintering area allows, then you can wait until spring before trimming. During the winter months, a lot of the branches and twigs will dry

out naturally and these have to be removed.

At the beginning of each new vegetation period in the spring, the structure of the plants must be reexamined to ensure the branches are stable. This is important, as they form the basic scaffolding for the masses of flowers that grow during the summer months. These are often very heavy. All weak branches and the soft winter growth must be removed.

Only prune within the flowering part of the plant.

Pruning to shape, training a standard

Normally, Angel's Trumpets grow into a bush. Their bushy appearance is often strengthened by numerous shoots coming from the ground. This growth shape is very popular, as it produces foliage that reaches almost to the ground and produces the first flowers at the earliest possible time. To encourage the formation of a bush, you should cut back all the shoots that are too long during the summer months. They can be used as cuttings for propagation.

Most Angel's Trumpets can also be trained as a standard. Grown thus, the crown is always the flowering part and this ensures that the plant produces its flowers as early as possible in each new vegetation period. Standards also need considerably less space to over-winter than the bushy plants that are often wide.

In order to train a young Angel's Trumpet to a standard, select the strongest shoot as the main stem and support it with a stable plant stake to guide it vertically upwards. If support is not given at the right time, the result will be standards that bend over or grow crookedly. In the worst case the whole top can break off. All side shoots and any that form in the future must be removed from the main shoot. You must also wait until the first flower bud has formed on the standard, then you can start work on the top. Allow side shoots to form above this shoot and support them. Shorten shoots that are too long and use as cuttings for propagation. Over the years a top will develop that is bushy and has lots of branches.

Planting out in summer

If you have the opportunity, you should try at least once to plant out large *Brugmansia* plants in summer. Usually they develop very quickly into imposing bushes covered in flowers — the aim of every *Brugmansia* enthusiast. If when they are planted out they receive a continual supply of both nutrients and water (see page 66), this is the easiest way to attain a result that is only achieved with intensive care if they are grown in containers.

Angel's Trumpets are planted out in April or May depending on the climate and over-wintering method used (see pages 69–71). The planting holes should be generously dug and carefully prepared. Angel's Trumpets demand a great deal of fertilizer and water, so the soil in the planting hole must have a high storage capacity for both nutrients and water.

If the soil contains loam, then it is sufficient to use the earth that is removed and just replace about two-thirds of it with compost, peat and slow-release fertilizers. If the soil is predominantly sandy, the proportion of peat or compost should be greater. It is important that at least 50 percent of the original soil is worked into the planting mix as otherwise the delicate exchange of water and nutrients between plant substrate and surrounding soil will be disturbed. This will produce an undesirable "tub effect" that cancels out the main advantage of planting out — namely a continuous supply of water and nutrients.

Before planting out it is a good idea to wrap the root ball with large-meshed wire netting to demarcate the form and size of the ball as this will assist the fall work of repotting. This wire basket allows the roots to grow through into the surrounding earth, and water and nutrients to be exchanged. In the fall, you can use the wire wall to dig out the ball that, still in its wrapping, can be lifted into its tub without effort.

General care during the summer months is about the same as for tub maintenance. You do not need to adhere so rigorously to the recommendations for watering and fertilizing. You will notice the positive result of the unhindered root growth in the soil as the plant finds new sources of food for itself.

In fall the plants are prepared for their winter quarters. As described above, the root ball can be dug out with a spade and lifted into a planter. The branches and twigs are pruned back either lightly or severely, depending on their summer growth. All the dead leaves and any fallen foliage should now be removed, otherwise they provide excellent hiding places for various plant pests. Snails in particular are easily taken into the overwintering room in this way. Now the Angel's Trumpet is ready to take up its allotted winter quarters.

Planting out saves a great deal of time when watering.

Over-wintering

Two very different over-wintering methods have proved practical for Angel's Trumpets:
1. Over-wintering in the cool where the aim is to stop growth completely during the winter months.
2. Over-wintering in the warm where the aim is for the plants to grow and flower but less vigorously.

Both methods of over-wintering need to be adapted to the growth behavior of the plants and to the existing temperatures before and after the plants are taken inside. In no way can both methods be combined. If a *Brugmansia*, which has over-wintered in the warm, is taken out at the time that would suit a plant that had over-wintered in the cold, it will definitely be damaged.

A cool cellar can be used for over-wintering.

Over-wintering in the cool

If Angel's Trumpets are only to be "brought through the winter" and not required to grow or flower at this time, then over-wintering in the cool is the answer. In this case the *Brugmansia* should be left outside during the fall for as long as possible. As temperatures go down slowly, the plants harden off and gradually become accustomed to slowing down. Generally, they should avoid a frost. Only *B. sanguinea* can withstand a few hours of temperatures below 26°F (-3°C).

Most of the leaves will have fallen off of their own accord. All the remaining leaves that are dead, withering or dried must be removed before the plant is taken inside. Prune back to healthy tissue the ends of those shoots that have frozen or died off. It is true the dead leaves will not cause a plant to die, but they considerably increase the risk of fungal and bacterial infections. Any kind of dying organic material provides an optimal nutritional base for these disease carriers. When an Angel's Trumpet has stopped growing completely, it is no longer in a position to stop the spread of infection by limiting the diseased tissue. In the worst case the whole plant will die.

Thoroughly cleaning the plant and tub before moving them inside helps to prevent any snails or other pests from being dragged inside. It is recommended that you examine the underside of the tub in particular, as snails and wood lice frequently get in through the drainage holes into the substrate. Whole nests of mice were once found in the huge tubs in the Herrenhäuser Garden. If you want to be quite certain that there are no uninvited winter guests, you should lift the ball of roots carefully out of the tub and examine the inner side of the tub. This must all be done before the first frost. By then, all the plants should have been taken into a cool room where the temperature is about 41°–50°F (5°–10°C), where the ventilation is good and that can be darkened if necessary. Angel's Trumpets will not usually need any water during their "winter sleep", though this depends on the humidity. You must, however, ensure that the ball of roots is never allowed to dry out completely. House interiors (68°–72°F/20°–22°C) are too warm only for *B. sanguinea* and *B. vulcanicola*. It is important that the plants have enough light to grow. The comparatively high temperatures will induce growth.

If the temperature stays within the recommended range of 41°–50°F (5°–10°C), this will prevent any winter growth. *B. insignis* is particularly fond of warmth and prefers the upper limit.

Angel's Trumpets kept over the winter in the cool should be brought outside as soon as possible in the following spring, but not until the main danger of frost is past. *Brugmansia* that have over-wintered in the cool seem to be able to tolerate cold temperatures really well. The more robust species such as *B. sanguinea* and *B. arborea* can even tolerate slight frosts overnight without suffering any permanent damage.

Over-wintering in the warm

Over-wintering in the warm has become more and more popular in recent times due to the resurgence of domestic conservatories and sunrooms. Angel's Trumpets like spending the cold part of the year in a conservatory.

B. sanguinea, which has always had the reputation of being a winter flower, shows itself at its full magnificence in the winter greenhouse. This allows the flower buds formed in fall to develop. If the plants over-winter in the cold and dark, these buds will dry and fall off.

Like *B. sanguinea*, the species *B. aurea*, *B. suaveolens*, *B.* x *candida*, *B. arborea* and many hybrids grow and flower all through the winter months at temperatures above 53°F (12°C).

Over-wintering *Brugmansia* in the warm is an option for owners of greenhouses.

The time of year when the plants are taken in and when they are brought out is especially important for plants that are going to over-winter in the warm. The aim here is not to persuade the Angel's Trumpets to stop growing, but exactly the opposite. They should keep growing, but at a reduced pace. Therefore, the optimal time to take them into the conservatory is when the average temperatures during the day sink to around 50°–53°F (10°–12°C).

The ideal conservatory for *Brugmansia* is light-filled, ventilated and has temperatures of between 53°–64°F (12°–18°C). As the growth of the plants here is only reduced compared to summer, rather than stopped, supplies of water and fertilizer must be adjusted to the changed conditions. This means that the plant is given about ¼ teaspoon (1.5 g or 1.5 mL) fertilizer per 1½ pints (1 liter) of water every week depending on how it is growing, plus moderate watering at other times.

The same factors that are important when the plant is taken inside apply to when it is moved out again. Avoid great differences in temperature between inside and outside. Normally, *Brugmansia* that have over-wintered in the warm are taken outside when all danger of frosts is past. An Angel's Trumpet that has over-wintered in the warm at 53°–64°F (12°–18°C) will definitely suffer if subjected to frosts at night.

As these plants have already sent out shoots in the warm conservatory, their new leaves are particularly sensitive to cold temperatures and also to direct sunlight. They should therefore be placed in a shady, sheltered position for the first weeks. It is a good idea to move them outside while it is raining. After a time, the Angel's Trumpets will have acclimatized again and they can safely be moved to their final, sunnier location.

Propagation

Propagation by cuttings is the primary method of propagating Angel's Trumpets. Usually cuttings root quickly with no problems and even small plants will flower after only a few months. Seedlings, on the other hand, need considerably more time until their first flowering, which takes place at the end of an immature phase.

With the exception of *B. arborea*, whose descendants show only slight variability — that is they are almost identical to their parents — the descendants of all the other species of *Brugmansia* vary considerably with regards to their inherited characteristics. Growers value this behavior, as it helps them to find new plants, but it frequently irritates *Brugmansia* enthusiasts who are hoping for a copy of the mother plant. They are forced to propagate vegetatively by cuttings.

Propagation by cuttings

When propagating by cuttings, the length of time before roots form and the number of cuttings which actually form roots varies from species to species of *Brugmansia*. Cuttings of *B. suaveolens*, *B. insignis* and *B. x candida* root quickly and easily, but cuttings of *B. vulcanicola*, *B. x flava* and various types of *B. versicolor* root slowly and have a high rate of failure. The other Angel's Trumpets fall somewhere in between.

Cuttings can be taken practically the whole year round, but the best results are obtained from those taken in spring and summer.

Both leafy tip cuttings and woody cuttings can be used. It is important that cuttings are taken, if possible, from the flowering part of the plants (see page 21). This will guarantee that the plants will flower and that they will flower while the plants are still young. Cuttings from the vegetative area of a *Brugmansia* are considerably slower to flower. Often the first flower will need a whole vegetation period before it forms.

Only cuttings from the flowering part of the plants promise early flowers.

When you are taking cuttings, your tools must be scrupulously clean for each cut. The plant sap can contain the most virulent viruses and these can easily be transferred to all the other cuttings. Not all species of *Brugmansia* display typical symptoms when they are attacked by a virus. Even apparently healthy plants can be infected. The knife should therefore be changed after each plant. In practice, knives should be metal and they should be cleaned after severing the cuttings, then put in the oven at a temperature of about 340°F (150°C) for an hour.

Dipping the knife into a solution containing 1 percent sodium solution or 5 percent sodium hypochlorite, contained in some household cleaners, can help to inactivate any viruses that may be present. These chemicals can also be used for cleaning any plant sap off the work area. To avoid

Brugmansia suaveolens hybrid 'Goldtraum', description on page 88.

transferring a virus, you must at all costs avoid bringing the cuttings from different mother plants into direct contact with each other.

Leafy cuttings should be about 6 in (15 cm) long. They put out roots after two to four weeks at temperatures around 68°F (20°C). Experiments have shown that dipping the cuttings into rooting powder with a content of 0.5 percent 3-indolebutyric acid accelerates the formation of roots by several days and improves the average rooting rate by 10 percent, on average. The cuttings are inserted to a depth of about 1½ in (3 cm) in a mixture of peat and sand. When propagating leafy cuttings, keep the humidity as high as possible and spread a clear plastic sheet over the propagation bed.

Woody cuttings, on the other hand, take longer to form roots and high humidity can cause rotting. Do not cover these with plastic.

Many species of *Brugmansia* will also root in water. Take cuttings about 6 in (15 cm) long and put in a glass with pure faucet water. It is important that only the lower 1½ in (2–4 cm) of the stalk is allowed to stand in the water. If the water is higher, then it will encourage the cutting to rot from the bottom up. After only a few days, depending on the species of *Brugmansia*, a white hard skin will form in areas on the part that is standing in the water. The first roots will shoot from these. After short peaks of roots sprout, put the cuttings into a small container with soil and spray frequently with water for the next few days. It can take a few weeks before an efficient root system has formed that is able to provide the plant with sufficient water.

A large quantity of plant material suitable for cuttings becomes available in fall when many *Brugmansia* are pruned back before being taken inside. All owners of greenhouses can now "mass produce" new plants. Woody cuttings, taken in fall, can be about 10 in (25 cm) long or even longer and should be placed in a mixture of peat and sand, in vermiculite or in pumice. Set the greenhouse temperature between 53°–64°F (12°–18°C). Many of these cuttings will form roots by the following spring. *B. vulcanicola, B. sanguinea* and *B.* x *flava* seem particularly suited to this "cool" root-forming. For root development the cuttings need the same light levels as for good growing conditions. If you use a hardwood cutting without a shoot tip, ensure that the lower part of the cutting is placed in the rooting mixture, and that it is not put in "head first".

It is a good idea to pot all cuttings into a nutrient-rich soil as soon as possible after they have formed roots. Once the cuttings have rooted they grow very quickly. If you want to cultivate a stately Angel's Trumpet, you should repot the young plants several times into bigger pots during the first year of cultivation.

Propagation by seed

There are various reasons why you should consider propagating Angel's Trumpets by seed. You can select seed from your "favorite plant" out of the young plants that are often genetically very different and, by growing from seed, you can also

build up new stock that will be almost virus-free. The fresh seed should be sown as early as possible, at temperatures between 64½°–79°F (18°–26°C). Cover the seed with approximately ⅕ in (4 mm) of humus, which must be kept wet.

The seed is relatively large and is pressed lightly into the humus to ensure contact with the moist planting mix. Initially cover the seed box with a glass plate to provide optimal humidity. At temperatures around 68°F (20°C), the various species of *Brugmansia* germinate very differently. As a rule, germination takes between 10 and 20 days. The young seedlings can then be planted out directly into small containers.

Young plants that are grown from seed go through an immature phase, easily recognized by the change in leaf shape. The plants do not reach flowering maturity until the end of this immature phase (see pages 20–22). The length of time before the first flowering varies with the species. On average, most *Brugmansia* flower for the first time when the plant is between 2½–5 ft (0.8–1.5 m) in size. If they are well cultivated, then they will usually reach this size in six to nine months.

Plants grown from seed can look very different. They differ not only in leaf shape and size, flower shape, color and size, but also in other traits, such as susceptibility to diseases or willingness to flower. The possibilities are almost endless and many interesting and valuable discoveries are undoubtedly waiting to be made. Just think of the diverse combinations that crossbreeding has already produced.

Cultivation

Growing new forms of Angel's Trumpets is both rewarding and interesting. As the seed of a single fruit can produce very different plants, each sowing produces new, often unknown types.

The decision on which of these new plants is actually new and suitable for propagating further is best left until after the first flowering. In order to keep the work up to this point to a minimum, all young plants can be planted out in one bed. This method reduces both the expenditure of care and keeps the need for space to a minimum.

Aims when cultivating new varieties

The various characteristics of the seed can be compared and the best types most easily selected from within stock that has been cultivated exactly the same way. When growing new varieties you should aim for the following qualities:

- a good variety should flower plentifully, have a lot of flowering phases per season outdoors and, if possible, no, or only short, non-flowering periods
- during the flowering season, flowers should form independent of the temperature
- the seedlings should produce their first flower as early as possible — that is, when they are still very small. Such plants, which branch early, usually have a compact structure
- shape and color of the flowers should be pleasing
- the individual flowers should last a long time and keep their shape and not collapse during the day, even when the weather is dry
- with regard to size, both large and small flowers are worth striving for, but the leaf size should always suit the flower size and the leaves should obstruct the flowers as little as possible
- the calyx should not be too large and should not cover too much of the colorful flower corolla
- both intensity and type of flower scent are worth striving for
- a good variety should be as resistant as possible to diseases

The last goal particularly should not be forgotten when selecting new varieties. Unfortunately, there are varieties in the existing range that are very susceptible to viruses. As the viruses that appear in *Brugmansia* are not transferred by the seed, it is recommended that healthy plants be bred by raising them from seed. From the seedlings of fruit from a diseased cultivar you should be able to select very similar types in flower shape and color.

When pollinating remember that, with the exception of *B. arborea*, all species are self-sterile. This means that you cannot pollinate between plants of the same inheritance. When plants that have been propagated by cuttings from the same mother plant (plants of the same variety) pollinate each other, they do not produce seeds that will germinate even though fruit does occasionally set.

This is why *Brugmansia*, in contrast to many other plant genera, successfully hybridize between the different species. The best result is a combination of the positive characteristics of two species. Thus, for example, *B.* x *flava* (hybridization of *B. arborea* with *B. sanguinea*) flowers during the summer months when *B. sanguinea* will not produce any flowers because the temperatures are too high.

The table below shows which species have been crossed with each other successfully. Some species hybridizations have still not succeeded; possibly the degree of intolerance between them is higher. Even in these cases, patience and luck may one day result in successful cross-pollinations.

In recent years numerous *Brugmansia* collectors in Germany, France, the U.S.A., Holland, Switzerland and Austria have proven that the growing of new improved hybrid forms is definitely possible. We now have flowers with a gigantic diameter of 10 in (26 cm) in glowing flower colors of rich pink-red, reddish orange and egg-yolk yellow. A rewarding result of extensive crossbreeding experiments has been types that are colored pink-blue-lilac with a metallic, shimmering sheen. Successfully crossing with a *B. arborea* hybrid helped *B. sanguinea*, which originally had no scent, to have a delicate pleasant perfume.

A large number of interesting plants have been recently grown. These successes promise even more surprises in the future.

In the Herrenhäuser Gardens, *Brugmansia* growers meet from time to time to enable the different growers to introduce their new discoveries to each other. As well as providing an opportunity for exchanging information, this gives growers the chance to exchange Angel's Trumpets. This is a circle of *Brugmansia* enthusiasts whose members have long been concerned with cultivating these beautiful plants.

Pollination

The technique of pollinating Angel's Trumpets can be described in a few words. Use a pair of long tweezers or a similar tool to remove the stamens, with the pollen, from the father plant and

Crossbreedings that have produced viable seeds

Female \ Male	B. arborea	B. aurea	B. x candida	B. x flava	B. insignis	B. sanguinea	B. suaveolens	B. versicolor	B. vulcanicola
B. arborea	x			x		x			x
B. aurea		x	x		x		x	x	
B. x candida		x	x		x		x	x	
B. x flava	x			x		x			x
B. insignis		x	x		x		x	x	
B. sanguinea	x			x		x			x
B. suaveolens		x	x		x		x	x	
B. versicolor		x	x		x		x	x	
B. vulcanicola	x			x		x			x

(x)   = crossbreedings that only occasionally produced seeds capable of germination
Female = mother plant
Male   = pollen giver

wipe these onto the stigma of the mother plant. As all *Brugmansia*, with the exception of *B. arborea*, are self-sterile the stamens do not need to be removed from the mother plant. There is no chance of self-pollination.

On *B. arborea*, on the other hand, because self-pollination is possible, all five stamens must be removed before the flower opens, by cutting through the flower wall. If this process is neglected or carried out too late, the result will be seed of a *B. arborea* that is identical.

Artificial pollination is best carried out immediately after a flower has opened; otherwise an insect will likely prove to be the faster pollinator. If you want to be quite certain of preventing this, then cover the stigma after pollination with a paper or foil wrapping to protect it from being pollinated by foreign agents.

How the fruit matures

You can tell whether pollination has been successful by looking at the flower stalk. It has not succeeded if it turns yellowish and begins to dry out, usually falling off with the calyx shortly after the dead flower corolla.

If on, the other hand, it stays green and full of sap and grows in length and width, then the pol-

Brugmansia arborea: The seed (left) is surrounded by a thick layer of cork that fills the whole of the inner part of the fruit even when it is dry (middle). When the fruit is cut open (right) you can see the typical structure of a *Brugmansia* fruit: a fleshy fruit wrap encloses two compartments with seeds.

lination was successful. A fruit is beginning to develop.

The dead flower corolla with the five stamens falls off in this case, too. The ovary, which is enclosed by the calyx, remains and stigma and style stay stuck to it for a long time. Depending on the species of *Brugmansia*, the calyx either dries out and falls off or it stays wrapped around the growing fruit like a dry skin.

The time the fruit takes to ripen also varies from species to species of *Brugmansia*. The ripe fruit begins to dry out from its lower end, becomes wrinkled and turns brownish in color. On *B. arborea* this occurs after just four months. At this point, the dark brown color of the seeds inside the fruit shows they are fully developed.

The fruits of *Brugmansia sanguinea* and *B. vulcanicola* need the longest time to ripen. They take up to eight months. In contrast to the other species, you cannot tell whether or not they are ripe from the outside, as their fruit casing remains green and does not dry out. Many a grower has not realized this and, with the best of intentions, left the fruit too long on the plant. After about nine months the seeds will begin to germinate. If they are still in the closed fruit they

Inner part of the fruit of *Brugmansia sanguinea* after the outer fruit husk has been removed. The seeds have a slightly developed corky husk and are not as tightly packed together as they are in *B. arborea*.

Fruits of *Brugmansia vulcanicola,* description page 90.

floury, fleshy, fruit wrapping as soon as the fruit is harvested. The seeds are like a three-dimensional puzzle of two oval-to-elongated seed packets (see page 77). You find this decorative way of arranging seeds only if you harvest them at the earliest possible time. After that the floury, fleshy, covering layer begins to dry out. The compactly arranged seed packets slowly loosen and fall apart. At this point the fruit covering yields slightly to outside pressure. *Brugmansia* must be harvested by this time at the latest, as it is now that the first seeds will start to germinate in the fruit.

Depending on the species, the fruit contains between 50 and 250 seeds. A lot of fruit produced by crossbreedings contain only a few seeds that are capable of germinating. Unfortunately, there is no external sign of whether or not seed is capable of germinating.

Brugmansia seeds can either be sown fresh or dried and packaged so that they are airtight. They can then be stored in a cool dry place for several years. When tests were carried out on five-year-old seed, it germinated almost as well as seed that had been freshly harvested.

After the seed has been dried, the cork-like seed shell can be removed. In many crossbreedings, a seed shell may develop but the embryo with its surrounding nutrient tissue will be missing.

Sometimes there will be a few viable seeds in the middle of a fruit with apparently no seed. To find these seeds and to bring them to germination is particularly interesting. It affords you the possibility of realizing a totally new hybridization combination.

will die. It is recommended, therefore, that when you are pollinating *B. sanguinea, B. vulcanicola* and their hybrids, you should note the time of pollination on a label and attach this to the flower stalk. Harvest time for the ripe seed will be eight months later.

Obtaining the seed

In its natural habitat the seed remains enclosed in the fruit until the outer skin has partially weathered. This can take months. In cultivation, however, the seed is released from the surrounding

Building a Brugmansia *collection*

The aim of many *Brugmansia* enthusiasts is to own a collection of *Brugmansia* plants that is as complete as possible and that contains every possible flower color and shape. Unfortunately, mainstream garden centers and flower shops usually offer only a small selection of different *Brugmansia*. To the enthusiast's annoyance, frequently only the flower color of the plants is given. When the plants are flowerless you cannot tell whether you already have the variety on offer or not. If the plants have been given a variety name you cannot always rely on it being the correct name. In comparing varieties it has been shown that the same plant type was available under up to five different names. And, conversely, completely different plants have often been given the same name.

Many *Brugmansia* collectors have been able to help themselves out of this dilemma. Using their own lists of varieties, they developed a lively exchange of cuttings. If someone has problems with cuttings, then for some time now many beautiful varieties have been available from specialist nurseries as young plants. They can buy these and will shortly have a larger collection.

A passion for collecting, exchanging cuttings and also the mainly vegetative propagation by gardening companies has inevitably resulted in an increased number of diseases. *Brugmansia* are not as robust as they are assumed to be. Almost none of the larger collections is completely virus-free. Many a *Brugmansia* enthusiast is not aware of this because numerous species and hybrids have no symptoms at all as long as they are grown under optimal conditions. They are unaware that the viruses are usually being passed on by cuttings. As there is no cure for a virus attack, except by tissue culture in a laboratory, the plant pathogen viruses in particular pose a serious problem for maintaining collections of Angel's Trumpets. It has been seen, even on varieties that are extremely resistant to viruses, that individual plants may occasionally show visible damage with growth depressions. To avoid the virus being transmitted further, plants that have been attacked must be destroyed. Over the years many of the older varieties have thus disappeared from collections.

On the other hand, increased interest in Angel's Trumpets has contributed enormously to the breeding of new varieties. Happily, the *Brugmansia* viruses do not seem to be carried in the seed and new healthy varieties soon fill the gaps left by the older ones. Moreover, many enthusiasts are spreading new varieties of their own with new names. The result is a plethora of variety classifications. What is confusing for the beginner is that for years the spectrum of possible colors and shapes of the flowers that result from hybridization between the few species has been well known. While the number of variety names has increased enormously, the variations of shape and colors of the flowers has basically remained the same. All hybridization is within the genetic possibilities of the genetic material inherited from the parent plants. Thus there are not expected to be considerable improvements in the intensity of color, in the color contrast in two-colored flowers, in the length of time the individual flowers will last, in the abundance of flowers, in the ability to set flowers all year-round or in the susceptibility to diseases. As these characteristics are already well represented, then new hybrids should aim to combine as many positive characteristics in one variety as possible.

The range of *Brugmansia* is subject to continual change for the most varied reasons. Apart from a few exceptions, it is almost impossible to describe a specific variety precisely. The flower color changes continually in the brief time from when the flower opens to when it is fully open. Flower color and flower size also depend to a large extent on temperature and nutritional condition. Descriptions of varieties and even photos taken by some *Brugmansia* enthusiasts are therefore often just a record of a particularly beautiful intermediary stage of the flowers. If a description of a variety is to be as dependable as possible then it should only be made if the weather conditions are at their optimum for the plant being described for as long a period as possible. The means that the heat-loving species such as *B. insignis* or *B. versicolor* should be evaluated only in the summer months and *B. sanguinea* and *B. vulcanicola*, which require cool temperatures, should be evaluated in fall, winter or spring.

A definite flowering stage should be used each time to evaluate the flower color. If a flower opens in the late afternoon of the first day then during the second day it will reach a phase of relatively constant color before it changes its color again on the third or fourth day as it fades. We therefore recommend that you view the typical color of a variety as that which the flowers show on the second day after the flower opens.

The range that we have listed does not try to list all the varieties of *Brugmansia* listed in catalogs or on the internet. We think it is important though, using examples, to provide information that is as comprehensive as possible on the variety of the types currently available with their varying flower shapes and colors. Every *Brugmansia* grower should try to catalog their new varieties into one of the following listed groups and give it the relevant name so that it can be related back to the parent species or the general group.

The *Brugmansia* range

B. arborea

Wild species with relatively small, creamy white flowers. Fruit is set by self-pollination. The species is relatively resistant to virus transferral.

B. arborea hybrids

Cultivated forms, most of which do not set fruit by self-pollination. The flowers are characterized by a calyx that is noticeably slit on one side with the split on the opposite calyx peak extending into the front half of the flower. The flowers are most frequently colored creamy white or yellow. Pink and red flowers are possible if it is crossed with *B. sanguinea* or *B. vulcanicola* . If you would like to grow small-flowered, non-rampant varieties, then you will reach your goal the fastest if you grow *B. arborea* hybrids.

Examples:

B. arborea hybrid 'Engelsglöckchen' Breeder unknown. Healthy variety with creamy white flowers that are about 8 in (21 cm) long. Flowers abundantly throughout the whole year.

B. arborea hybrid 'Mini Star' Bred by A. Kirchner-Abel (Duisburg). It has small, greenish white

The small-flowered *Brugmansia arborea* hybrid 'Sternchen' next to red-flowering fuchsias.

flowers (length 5 in [12cm], crown diameter 2 in [5cm]). It is not a strong grower.

B. arborea hybrid 'Sternchen' A variety that grows outwards. It has small, creamy to yellow-ish-colored flowers about 7 in (18 cm) long. This variety flowers abundantly and was developed from a cross between *B.* x *flava* with *B. arborea*.

B. aurea

The varieties listed in the group are cultivated forms with the character of the wild species. They have white, yellow or pink flowers that are of average size and trumpet-shaped.

Examples:

B. aurea 'Goldenes Kornett' Beautiful selection of the wild species with golden-yellow flowers. It flowers relatively well.

B. aurea 'Rotkirch' Originally grew in the wild in Colombia. Has very beautiful pink flowers that turn reddish as they fade. Does not have many flowers.

Brugmansia aurea 'Tufino'

B. aurea 'Tufino' From Ecuador. Has beautifully shaped, white flowers with a fairly firm consistency. Unfortunately, this *B. aurea* tends to produce more vegetation than flowers.

B. aurea hybrids

Many of these cultivated forms have retained the basic characteristics of *B. aurea*, particularly the shape of the flower corolla. In cases of doubt, the shape of the fruit will decide whether a plant is a genuine wild species or a hybrid. Hybridization always results in a more elongated fruit shape than the fruit of *B. aurea*.

The *B. aurea* hybrid 'Culebra' is the most strikingly different. It has not yet been finally clarified whether this variety actually does belong to the small group of *B. aurea* (compare also the description of the Indian forms of *B. aurea* on pages 33–34).

Examples:

B. aurea hybrids 'Amaron' and 'Quinde' Indian varieties from Colombia. They have white flowers. They bloom in bursts and on the whole have few flowers. The leaves are elongated and divided irregularly.

B. aurea hybrid 'Citronella' Bred by H. Blin (Strassburg). Has lemon-yellow flowers that are 7 in (18 cm) long. Flowers well.

B. aurea hybrid 'Culebra' Indian variety from Colombia. The white flowers have deep splits between the flower peaks and give the impression that the flower corolla has not developed. Does not produce many flowers. The leaves are unusually narrow and give the variety its unmistakable appearance.

B. aurea hybrid 'Rosabelle' Hybrid by H. Blin (Strassburg) of a *B. aurea* wild variety with *B.* x *candida* 'Ocre'. The pink flowers reach a length of 13 in (34 cm). The flower corolla is evenly colored throughout.

B. aurea hybrid 'Rosamund' An intensely colored, pink-flowered variety bred by H. Blin (Strassburg). It has long peaks on the edges of its petals.

Hybrids from B. aurea x B. suaveolens

The shape of the flowers of these hybrids is somewhere in the middle between both parents. The peaks are often very distinct. The flowers range from white through yellow to pink. Hybrids of *B. aurea* and *B. suaveolens* frequently inherit their strong growth with large leaves from *B. aurea*. They inherit their long-lasting flowers from *B. suaveolens*.

Examples:

B. hybrid 'Gelber Riese' Bred by B.-J. Herder (Rudolstadt). Has light yellow flowers that are 10 in (26 cm) long.

Above: *Brugmansia* hybrid 'Weisse Krone'
Right: *B.* x *candida* 'Ocre'

B. hybrid 'Weisse Krone' Bred by Herrenhäuser Gardens. Has creamy white flowers that are 12½ in (32 cm) long.

B. x *candida* (hybrids from *B. aurea* x *B. versicolor*)

The flower shape and size of these hybrids is somewhere in the middle between their two parents. They usually have more flowers than either. The double-flowering varieties are particularly popular. Starting with the very old variety 'Tutu' with its white flowers, there are double-flowering varieties in yellow, apricot or pink.

Examples:

B. x **candida 'Esmeraldas'** One of the hybrids found by A. Holguin (Quito, Ecuador). It has reddish pink flowers that are 11½ in (29 cm) long.

B. x **candida 'Grand Marnier'** Old variety from the "Les Cédres" garden of J. Marnier-Lapostolle (St. Jean, Cap-Ferrat, France). It was sold com-

mercially at the beginning of the last century by the firm of Hillier, England. Its flowers range from a pale brownish color to apricot.

B. x *candida* **'Ocre'** The original 'Ocre' variety comes from the Kamsa Indians in Colombia. It has golden-yellow pendulous flowers that have a particularly beautiful shape. Probably most of the current hybrids that have golden-yellow flowers inherited their color from the variety 'Ocre'.

Hybrids have now been bred that look identical. These have replaced the variety that became susceptible to disease because of long-term vegetative propagation.

Above: *B.* x *candida* 'Rosea'. Top right: *Brugmansia* x *candida* f. *variegata* 'Maya'. Right: Almost all double-flowering *Brugmansia* can be traced back to *B.* x *candida* f. *plena* 'Tutu'.

***B.* x *candida* 'Rosea'** A hybrid collected by A. Holguin in Quito, Ecuador. It has pale pink flowers.

***B.* x *candida* f. *plena* 'Perfektion'** New hybrid bred by A. Kirchner-Abel (Duisburg, Germany) in 2000. It has pink double flowers.

***B.* x *candida* f. *plena* 'Tutu'** A variety that has been in cultivation for a long time. It has a double, white flower corolla. Unfortunately, many of the plants of this variety in collections are diseased with a virus.

***B.* x *candida* f. *variegata* 'Maya'** This variety comes from France. It has light apricot flowers and its leaves are variegated greenish white, mainly along the edges.

Cooler fall temperatures produce greenish flowers on this yellow *Brugmansia sanguinea*.

"You have come at the wrong time of day," is what we would like to reply. "In the early evening the Solanaceae path in the Baroque Garden is trans-formed into a veritable paradise of scent." In their natural habitat, most Angel's Trumpets are pollinated by night moths and the intoxicating perfume of the flowers is intended for them alone. *Brugmansia* open their new flowers from late afternoon right through into the evening hours.

As a burst of flowers are opening, this *B. versicolor* temporarily has both pale yellow as well as apricot flowers.

During this time each individual flower emits such a strong scent that it carries a long way; its aim is to direct the insects along the right path.

Change in position of leaf

During the evening hours *Brugmansia* change in other ways. Like a lot of other plants, Angel's Trumpets adopt a typical sleep position at this time of day. The leaves around the tips of the growing shoots change from being horizontal to pointing almost vertically upwards. In this way they protect the extremely sensitive vegetation point from losing too much heat during the night. After sunrise, in the early hours of the morning, the leaves move back into their horizontal position (see photos opposite).

In the early hours of the evening this *Brugmansia suaveolens* displays its impressive color change from yellow through white to pink.

Above: *Brugmansia* x *flava:* before nightfall the leaves take up their "sleep position". Above right: *B.* x *flava:* Position of the leaves around the tips of the shoots during the day.

Changes in the position of the flower buds

A puzzle that still has to be solved is the way the flower buds move while they are developing into flowers. During the first phase the flower buds of *Brugmansia* always stand upright. As they get bigger they turn more and more downwards until finally they are hanging down in a perpendicular position. The flowers of *B. versicolor* have now reached their final position, but *Brugmansia* with a nodding to horizontal flower position have not. Particularly on *B. suaveolens* you can clearly see that before the flowers are fully open, they turn slightly upwards again against the force of gravity (see photo right).

Right: *B. versicolor* hybrid f. *plena:* As the flower buds get bigger they rotate 180°.

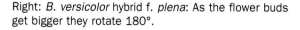

95

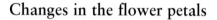

Changes in the flower petals

Frequently, *Brugmansia* will be seen with flowers that have varying numbers of petals. There will be flowers with four or six petals or peaks as well as normal five-petaled flowers. Flowers with as many as ten petals growing into a corolla have been seen (see photo above left). Naturally they draw all the attention to themselves because of the enormous diameter of their flowers. The proud grower who sees such a phenomenon in the first flower of a seedling hopes that all the other flowers will look the same. Unfortunately this will not be the case. An increase in the number of flower petals that grow together into one corolla is not a stable characteristic of Angel's Trumpets. The doubling of the flower corolla in double-flowering varieties is, however, usually very dependable. There will be types though that have both double and single flowers on the same plant.

Brugmansia can also have stunted flower petals. During the six months of winter many petals of the *B. aurea* hybrid 'Culebra' are reduced to short, dark green, string-like shapes. It is astonishing that the development of the stamens is not

Above: Incomplete flowers next to a normally formed flower on *Brugmansia aurea* 'Tufino'.
Above left: *B.* hybrid: on the same plant you often find flowers with a larger number of peaks as well as normal five-peaked flower corollas.

affected, which gives the whitish anthers the most striking appearance (see page 97).

Now and then on *B.* x *flava*, the flower buds will only grow to about $1/4$ in (5 mm) in size. Within the tiny buds the anthers will be incompletely developed. When development is nearly complete, the peaks of the tiny calyx sepals will tip outwards. This is apparently a sign to the opening mechanism of the calyx.

Sometimes irregularities occur even on flowers that are fully grown. Normally formed blooms appeared on a *B. aurea* 'Tufino' next to ones whose petals were partly reduced so that the malformed corolla had decorative holes (see photo above).

Changes in size of flowers and leaves

The winter flowers of almost all *Brugmansia* species that bloom during the winter months in the conservatory are a third to a quarter smaller than their comparable summer flowers. In contrast, many leaves are a third to a quarter larger in area during their winter growth. The size of the leaf depends greatly on the amount of nutrients available.

Change in flowering behavior

Flower development in most of the *B. sanguinea* types is inhibited by high summer temperatures. Even flower buds that have formed will be dropped. This species does produce exceptional cases where flowers are also formed during the warm summer months, but the calyx frequently opens so late that the flower is already badly damaged. The flower corollas are often rolled and folded together, and appear stunted and only partially formed. In the fall the calyxes on the same plants will open at the right time once again and completely normal flowers will develop.

Unfortunately, various experiments where *B. sanguinea* has been crossed with *B. arborea* have shown that the characteristic of a non-opening calyx can be inherited. In some otherwise very beautiful types of plants this can be very marked. In these cases the calyx must be opened at the right time by hand, otherwise the flower's growth within the calyx will be stunted and it will die. The easiest way to open the calyx is to very carefully tear the peak. Opening the calyx early does not seem to harm the development of the flower in any way.

Flower edge drying out

Some Angel's Trumpets with thin-walled flower corollas, such as *B. suaveolens* and *B. x insignis*, will produce types with a very unattractive characteristic. Shortly after the bud blossoms the flower will begin to dry out from the lower rim.

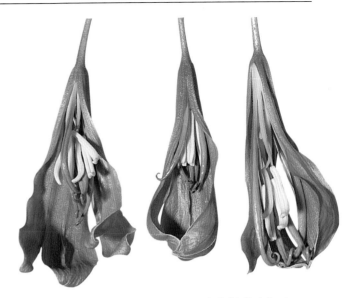

Winter flowers of *Brugmansia aurea* hybrid 'Culebra' with green string-like flower petals.

Leaves turning yellow and dropping

Unfortunately, over the whole cultivation period, large quantities of leaves continually or at intervals turn yellow and are dropped. Leaves will tend to fall if the plant is lacking nutrients. Angel's Trumpets were originally inhabitants of the equatorial zone and, as such, are not subject to the strict rest and growth phases that are prescribed elsewhere by the change from winter to summer and vice versa. Thus, leaves do not fall at one single time in the fall in cooler regions with distinct seasons. *Brugmansia* are continually putting on new growth and are therefore continually dropping the used leaves that are no longer of use to the plant. This characteristic may not be endearing to the plant enthusiast but cannot be prevented by any special cultivating measures.

As has been mentioned previously, however, types of Angel's Trumpets can develop whose foliage stays green for a long time and is hardly dropped at all. It will be up to plant growers in the future to make this totally desirable characteristic more widespread.

Diseases and pests

If you own only a few Angel's Trumpets then you will seldom have serious problems with diseases or pests. The more comprehensive the collection becomes, however, the greater the likelihood that pests and diseases will appear.

Individual species and varieties vary in their sensitivity to diseases and pests. While *B. arborea* and *B. aurea* have proven to be the most resistant species, if they are cultivated under conditions that are particularly attractive to pests and diseases, where they are continually subjected to attack, then they too will finally succumb. Spin mites are frequently found on plants that are cultivated against the wall of a house under eaves where it is dry and warm.

Usually a slight attack of thrips, whitefly, aphids or cicadas does not do too much damage to a *Brugmansia*; the fast-growing Angel's Trumpet will easily recover from the light damage done by their sucking activity. In a stock of plants grown in containers, though, it needs just one plant with a virus for even the mildest attack by these pests to have fatal consequences. It is extremely likely that the virus will be transferred to all the other *Brugmansia* and, as a virus attack cannot be cured, then you will probably lose all the infected plants.

This is why plants should always be cultivated under conditions where the likelihood of catching an infection or attracting pests is as low as possible. Here the motto "Prevention is better than cure" definitely applies.

If, however, a "cure" is necessary then you should go to the nearest plant protection office and get information on the latest pest control methods available. These could include using useful insects or spraying with chemical pesticides. Because the marketing of these preparations is constantly being reviewed both by the manufacturers and for legal purposes, we will not name any individual preparations.

Optimal cultivation conditions protect against diseases and pests.

Viral diseases

B. sanguinea and its hybrids, *B.* x *flava* and *B.* x *candida* are the most susceptible to virus attacks. Virus-sick plants do not occur only among cultivated plants. In their native habitats *Brugmansia*, *B. sanguinea* in particular, are attacked by the most varied viruses. A virus was discovered on *B. sanguinea* and *B.* x *candida* in the Sibundoy Valley in Colombia, South America, and was given the name Colombian Datura Potyvirus. Other viruses that have been isolated from *Datura* or *Brugmansia* include Datura wilt virus, Datura distortion mosaic virus, Datura quercina virus, Datura rugose leaf-curl virus and Datura malformation virus. This list is definitely not complete but it is impressive and shows that the

Brugmansia x *candida*: The mosaic-like virus symptoms reveal themselves first on the young leaves.

Brugmansia sanguinea: In a major attack the virus disease moves into the flowers as well.

former *Datura* now classified as *Brugmansia* are host plants for numerous viruses. This makes them important subjects for investigation for virus research where they are used to prove the existence of viruses.

The symptoms of viral diseases can take many forms. Usually an infection appears first on the leaves around the tips of the shoots. A mosaic-type pattern of light and dark green spots is the most frequent symptom. In later stages the color contrast of the mosaic pattern increases and the dark green spots that are found between the leaf blades bulge out irregularly. In a particularly fierce attack the disease moves on to the flowers as well. They too will then have the typical mosaic-type spotting combined with a distinct greening of the corolla tube. By this stage you will notice that the newest leaves are very stunted and the growth pattern of the plant is already inhibited. Root growth is also affected. It is an established fact that cuttings from *B. sanguinea* or *B.* x *flava* affected by a virus do not form roots.

If virally sick plants are provided with an optimal amount of water and nutrients during the summer vegetation period, they can remain without any signs of disease. Many a buyer of the double-flowering variety *B.* x *candida* 'Tutu' will have had this experience as, unfortunately, this variety is often virally infected. Plants grown in the conservatory under optimal conditions seldom show outward signs of the disease. Not until the beginning of winter when the plants reduce their growth does the unmistakeable mosaic-like pattern begin to appear on the leaves.

Some years the symptoms of the disease that produces a mosaic-like spotting on the leaves are weaker; in others, they are stronger. This see-saw variation, however, does not usually cause the plant to die, as *Brugmansia* seem to be able to live with the virus.

It is a different story with a disease that is said to be produced by the tomato-spotted wilt virus.

Brugmansia sanguinea: Such necrotic spots on the stalks can be a symptom of the tomato-spotted wilt virus.

Initially, brownish necrotic spots appear on the stalks. Within a few days the parts of the stalks above the spots wither and die off. Emergency shoots appear on the branches that are still alive, but they are very weak and their leaves have an irregular pattern of pale green and normal green zones. Within just a few weeks this disease will definitely kill the plant.

Until now this fatal viral infection has only been seen in collections that were cultivated during the winter in a conservatory where it was light and warm. This is no surprise really, because this is the one place where carriers of the tomato-spotted wilt virus are active throughout the year.

These carriers are various species of thrips, particularly the Californian blossom thrips (*Frankliniella occidentalis*) and the apple thrips (*Thrips tabaci*). When the larvae of the thrips suck the sap from the plant, they take the virus with it. In extreme cases they can carry the virus with them and continue passing it to other plants for the rest of their lives.

These insects are tiny; the brownish colored adult creatures are only $\frac{1}{8}$ in (1.5 mm) long. Their size and their secretive way of life make them difficult to find.

You can assume that they are present in almost every greenhouse. If you hang up sticky blue tablets you will find the Californian blossom thrips. They are attracted to this color, fly onto the tablet and then become stuck to the sticky surface. This is one way of determining whether you have the pest and also the first line of attack. However, if thrips are present in particularly large numbers you should consider spraying with a suitable insecticide.

Fighting virus carriers is one of the most important ways of preventing the spread of viral diseases. The major viral carriers, including thrips, that attack *Brugmansia* are aphids, whitefly and cicadas. The viruses are not only transferred within the container plant stock. When the plants are put outside for the summer, viruses can be transferred from sick plants in the garden.

Viruses can be transferred by mechanical methods, such as wounding the outer skin by breaking a plant hair. You should never touch a healthy plant after you have had contact with a sick one, as hands or gloves can transfer minute quantities of infected plant sap. Viral diseases are easily spread when propagating by cuttings. If the knife used to sever the cutting comes in contact just once with the sap of a sick plant, it becomes an ideal source of infection for all subsequent cuttings.

Being scrupulous about hygiene when propagating, selecting healthy mother plants, and destroying all virally infected plants but never putting them on the compost, are all proven measures for fighting viruses. The point is to avoid catching the virus in the first place, as plants that have once caught the virus cannot be cured with traditional methods. When plants are particularly valuable you can seek the help of a laboratory. They have specialized tissue culture techniques and by isolating a microscopically small meristeme of the tip of the shoot they can obtain virus-free plants from a variety that has become infected.

Fungal diseases

Recently, *Brugmansia* are becoming more and more frequently infected by diseases that apparently are caused by harmful fungi. Currently, there is not sufficient information available about either the pathogenic agents or how to fight them. Only the symptoms of the disease can be described here.

Stalk wilt

Stalk wilt is a disease that must be taken extremely seriously. *B. suaveolens* and all its hybrids are particularly susceptible. Initially, waxy blackish spots appear on the branches. These gradually dry out and turn light brown. The spots first extend longitudinally along the shoots, but can also gradually take over the whole stalk area. The edges of the leaves on the affected parts of the plant roll under and become brittle. In extreme cases the affected parts fall off.

Investigations seem to indicate that species of fungi from the genera *Phoma* or *Verticillium* could be the cause. Initial observations show that they can be checked by repeated spraying with the fungicides Rovral or Ronilan.

Leaf spot disease

A leaf spot disease can attack individual *Brugmansia* within a few days and as it runs its course a large number of leaves die. Dark green roundish spots with a light middle appear on these leaves. Gradually these spots dry out and become brown. The dry tissue can break off and leaves bare spots behind. As it continues, the leaves dry out more and more, curl under and finally fall off. The plants recover by new growth, but within a few weeks are attacked by the disease again.

Pests

Leaf bugs

The green leaf bug (*Lygus pabulinus*) apparently has a great liking for *Brugmansia* and for all varieties and hybrids of *B. suaveolens*, in particular. From the beginning of July until well into August, the warmest time of the year, these insects can cause considerable and very unsightly damage to Angel's Trumpets growing outside, particularly to young leaves and the tips of shoots that are still soft.

At the beginning of the attack only tiny yellowish- to brownish-colored spots are visible. These insignificant puncture spots are initially unimportant but they greatly inhibit normal leaf growth. The bug's saliva is poisonous to the plants and causes the leaves to grow irregularly and to be completely deformed. Sometimes by this stage there will be no more leaf bugs on the *Brugmansia* and you will look in vain for the pest that is apparently "eating like mad".

But even when leaf bugs are present, it is difficult to find them. They occur only in limited numbers and stay well hidden. During the day they are extremely lively. As soon as you get near them the larvae disappear like lightning onto the protective underside of the leaf or between the young leaves of the tip of the shoot. The adult insects fly away or simply fall to the ground. A search in the early hours of the morning is often more successful. The leaf bugs have not yet regained their full mobility after the cool of the night.

The adult green leaf bug is a six-legged, rather flat insect. It is yellowish green in color and up to ¼ in (5 mm) long with two pairs of wings that lie close to the body. Its larva, which at first sight looks like a giant aphid, is almost as big.

Warm dry years provide particularly favorable conditions for leaf bugs to multiply. Methods of control only succeed if they are carried out early, even before the bugs begin their sucking activity. This is why you need to spray during the cool morning hours with a suitable insecticide. At this time the leaf bugs, which are usually so lively, have not regained their full speed and are sitting quietly on the undersides of the leaves.

Unfortunately, a single spraying can never guarantee success. You will have to monitor continually and be ready for a new influx of creatures from the neighborhood at any time.

In a severe attack the leaves can dry out and fall off.

To control them you will need to spray with an acaricide at regular intervals, ensuring that you spray both the larvae and the eggs as well as the adults.

Spider mites

Spider mites can become extremely unpleasant pests while the plants are over-wintering in the conservatory and during their summer stay outside. During the warm summer months, placing plants under overhanging eaves where they are protected from humidity provides the mites with favorable conditions for multiplying. They are infinitesimal but very soon spread from the undersides of leaves to the young leaves at the tips of the shoots and cover them with their fine webs.

Spider mites pierce the leaf tissue and suck the cells out. This causes shimmering spots to form. These are silver to light yellow in color and gradually spread to cover the whole surface of the leaf.

Aphids

There are hundreds of species of aphid and many are found on *Brugmansia*; however, these piercing-sucking pests only cause severe damage if they cover tips of the shoots thickly. Angel's Trumpets are such strong growers that a mild attack of aphids does not usually produce any visible damage on the plants. If the aphids are carrying a viral disease then it is a much more serious matter.

Whitefly (moth shield aphid)

Whitefly are mainly greenhouse pests as only there can they over-winter. They move outside in the spring with the container plants and if the summer is warm and dry they multiply and become a particularly unpleasant pest. The insects

Above left: Yellow spotting on leaves from spider mites. Above right: Leaf deformations from leaf bugs on *Brugmansia suaveolens*. Opposite left: *Brugmansia suaveolens*: Symptoms of stalk wilt are light brown spots surrounded by a waxy blackish edge. Opposite right: Leaf spot disease on *Brugmansia* x *flava*.

are up to $\frac{1}{8}$ in (1.5 mm) in size. They usually sit on the undersides of the leaves and their white wings make them easy to recognize. The sucking damage is similar to that of the spider mites, but the spots are noticeably larger.

Caterpillars and snails

Frequently, damage by "genuine" chewing insects is also seen on Angel's Trumpets. Caterpillars and snails are the main culprits. The damage is typically holes, which are quite large, on leaves and flowers that were previously completely intact. You should not underestimate the ability of snails to cover large distances. During the day they usually hide under or in the container (in the overwintering quarters as well) and only leave at night to look for food. Their tracks can be traced back along the trail of slime.

Non-parasitic diseases

Cork

Cork growths occur on a variety of ornamental plants. They are usually caused by high humidity, a metabolic disturbance, or the sucking activity of mites or thrips.

These causes seem less likely for the cork growths on *Brugmansia*, but as yet no concrete indicator has been found for why they do form.

Normally the bark on the trunks of *Brugmansia* remains completely smooth even as it ages; it does not break on the surface as on other trees. Cork growths start as round spots that bulge up and become callused. Sometimes you will see a severe cork formation even on the older parts of the trunks of Angel's Trumpets. Their trunks start to look very like the bark of the Sakhalin Cork Tree (*Phellodendron amurense*). On a *Brugmansia* this cork formation is not the normal thickening of the trunk. It is apparently a symptom of a disease that affects the thickness and the longevity of the trunks that are infected. *B. suaveolens* and its hybrids are the most susceptible.

Dátura

Datura — *magical, medicinal plant for everyone*

An Indian legend tells the story of *Datura*. "Long, long ago a brother and sister lived deep in the earth. The boy was called A'neglakya and the girl was called A'neglakyatsi'tsa. The two of them often came to the surface of the earth and wandered around. They took note of everything and reported what they had seen and heard to their mother. This did not please the divine twin sons of the sun father. When they met A'neglakya and A'neglakyatsi'tsa one day, they asked them: 'How are you?' 'We are happy,' answered the pair. They told the divine pair how they could make people fall asleep or see ghosts, become noisy and restless and to recognize who had committed a crime. After this meeting the divine pair were in agreement that A'neglakya and A'neglakyatsi'tsa knew too much and they banished them forever to the inner part of the earth. Flowers appeared at the place where the children climbed down. These were exactly the same flowers that they had worn on their foreheads when they visited the earth. The divine pair named the plant A'neglakya after the name of the boy. Since that time numerous children have scattered this original plant all over the earth. Some of their flowers are yellowish, some colored reddish or blue like the colors of the four points of the compass."

Not all peoples described the history of the development of the *Datura* as poetically as the

Previous pages: *Datura inoxia* in a front garden, description pages 117–119.

Zuñi Indians described their *Datura inoxia*. Its use as a medicament and hallucinogen has been known worldwide for centuries.

Wide variations in alkaloid concentrations make *Datura* very difficult to use as a medicament.

Nearly all parts of the *Datura* plant were used. Like many of the other nightshade plants they contain high concentrations of the various tropane alkaloids such as scopolamine, hyoscayamine or atropine. Both the overall alkaloid content and its composition are dependent on the age of the plant, where it is growing and the weather, which can cause variations. Sunshine plays a very important part. *Datura* from tropical zones can contain four to five times more effective substances than that growing in northern countries. Within the plant the highest concentrations of alkaloid are found in the flowers and the seeds. Leaves, roots and sprouting parts have a much lower content.

The wide variations in the concentrations of contents make *Datura* very difficult to use as a medicament. It is crucial that dosages are exact when using such highly poisonous plants. The user needs to have a great deal of experience and detailed plant knowledge so that no harm results from using it. Those who are skilled in the use of herbs, therefore, were highly respected by the populace in areas where *Datura* grew naturally.

106

They used *Datura* as an effective painkiller against feverish illnesses, in treating tumours, chest infections, skin diseases, and as a cure against mental illness.

Even today the various *Datura* species are still used for medicinal purposes. Scopolamine, obtained from the dried leaves, is used by the pharmaceutical industry as a base substance for spasmolytica.

The various *Datura* species have gained major importance from their ability to produce visual hallucinations. When people took *Brugmansia* they could only explain the change in consciousness by attributing it to the influence of supernatural divine powers. They believed the same of *Datura*. It was only a step to making the *Datura* itself into a divine plant. In India, the presumed native habitat of *Datura metel,* dhatura was dedicated to the Hindu god Shiva, the god of destruction. In China, where *Datura* had been introduced from India between the Sung and Ming dynasties (A.D. 960–1644), the story was told that while Buddha was giving his sermons the sky had sprinkled all the *Datura* plants with drops of dew or rain.

But in the New World, too, the characteristics of the native *Datura* species were highly esteemed. Schultes and Hofmann (1980) wrote of the tribe of the Tubatulobal:

"Boys and girls drink *Datura* at puberty to 'reach life' and adults used the plant to help them have visions. They softened the roots in water and let them steep for ten hours. The young people drink huge quantities of this brew and then fall into a dazed state which is accompanied by hallucinations that can last up to 24 hours.

If an animal appears in these visions, for example an eagle or a hawk, then it becomes the person's 'favourite animal' or their spiritual talisman for the rest of their lives.

If on the other hand he catches a glimpse of 'life' then he has gained a guardian spirit. Because this spirit is immortal it can appear at any time it is wanted. Children may never kill the 'favourite animal' which has appeared to them in the *Datura* vision. It can be summoned to visit a patient who is seriously ill and can bring about a cure."

Even today *Datura* is attributed such strong power by many Indian tribes that only someone "who has the power" can control them. For this reason only the medicine man or a healer is allowed to take "the magic plant". Only at rare ceremonies, such as the initiation ritual described above, may ordinary members of the tribe be allowed into the divine trance by taking *Datura*.

A majority of the population feels a ritual reverence towards the *Datura*. Others, though, are not afraid to misuse the extraordinary properties of this plant for their own purposes, which are often even criminal.

In 1949 Reko wrote in his work on "Magic Poisons" about the neighborhood of Guanajuato, Mexico, and of the "chain smokers" who commonly smoked cigarettes that were a mixture of dried toloachi leaves and tobacco. Toloa is the Aztec term for "nod the head" and alludes to the nodding movement of the *Datura* fruit: "It first produces quickening of the pulse, the heart starts pounding, head becomes tight, walk becomes unsteady, in short what is called a 'dry drunkenness'. Repeating the dose over a period causes hallucinations and finally leads to a trance ... those who are affected lurch around weak and listless — like those drunk on alcohol — as long as they are sober, and become upright and sprightly and regain their old strength as soon as they take the poison again. Later a light but continuous stupidity sets in which then turns into a kind of deafness. It takes a while to grasp what is being said, unwillingness and irritability set in then finally there is complete apathy against the world. The Yaqui Indians call such people Hiepsa-mucuchim, which means a living corpse. It is a very apt description. The spirit is completely dead while the body continues to live."

In this connection it is interesting that Wade Davis (1985), in his research into the voodoo cult on Haiti, came across a food that they gave the "zombie", which is an African word for a will-less tool of a magician. This is a soup that is made of sweet potatoes and sugar beet syrup, but mainly of *Datura stramonium*. In Creole this plant is very aptly described as "zombie cucumber". In India, the Thugs were a sect that honored the goddess Kali and lived from stealing. They were notorious for inviting travelers to a meal, usually a hot curry. Ground Thorn Apple seeds were mixed into the food. Once the victims were drugged in this way they were incapable of reacting and could easily be robbed.

In different regions of India *Datura* was a popular poison for suicide and murder. Between 1950 and 1965 the State Chemical Laboratories in Agra alone investigated 2778 deaths that were caused by species of *Datura*.

At the beginning of the 15th century *Datura* found its way to western Europe. It is likely that the first plants were part of the baggage of groups of Sinte and Rom peoples. The name "gypsy weed" is common today for the Thorn Apple. In some regions they attributed *Datura* with special powers and scattered their seeds to keep away demons. The horse dealers, too, knew the sales promotional effect of these plants: "Even the most miserable old nag would become as fiery as a thoroughbred, if you put a few rolled up leaves into its rectum" (Frohne and Pfander, 1982).

Datura became even better known as an essential ingredient of numerous witch's brews and love potions. The Thorn Apple belongs to the classic witch's weeds along with deadly nightshade (*Atropa belladonna*), henbane (*Hyoscyamus niger*) and mandrake (*Mandragora officinarum*). Its leaves and seeds were smoked as an aphrodisiac or ground up and made into bath salts, magic powders, salves and pomades.

A love potion, which was prepared with toloache, was said to perform miracles. It has kept its reputation; Mexico's Santo Toloache, formerly a heathen saint, is revered today in Christian clothes in many a village church. According to tradition he helps to waken love in the desired object.

Naturally the stories told here about *Datura* are only a fraction of all the stories, myths and legends that have gathered over the centuries. The different recipes for ointments, medicinal powders and love potions alone would fill a book. They all help to demonstrate the great importance that was attached to the Thorn Apple in the past.

There is such reverence for its outstanding properties that perhaps it is also understandable that the question of where this plant genus originally came from has become secondary. Very recently, doubts were raised as to whether *Datura metel* was in fact the only one to originate in the Asiatic or African region. It can be proven that all the other *Datura*, like all the *Brugmansia*, come from the New World.

According to an age old Tao legend, the original name of the plant, which we know today as *Datura metel*, is the name of a Pole star. All the ambassadors from this star who were sent to the earth carried one of its flowers in their hand. This is why people eventually gave the plant the name of the star.

Opposite: In 1613 in the Great Herbarium of Basilius Besler — Hortus Eystettensis — *Datura stramonium* was listed as "hedgehog's prickles" or "spiky nut".

Form and structure of Thorn Apples

Brugmansia and *Datura* are very similar in their structure — which is not surprising for they are closely related. The form and structure of *Brugmansia* was described in detail on pages 20–23. The special additional features of *Datura* can be best understood if they are compared with the properties that have already been described. At the same time, a comparison will clarify why *Brugmansia* and *Datura* are two different genera (see page 10, "*Brugmansia* and *Datura* — what is the difference?").

The distinctive juvenile phase in *Brugmansia* begins after the seed has germinated and ends with the formation of the first flower. This phase is much shorter in a *Datura*. First, the two linear-shaped germinating leaves form, then as soon as about four foliage leaves have formed, the tip of the shoot can be changed into a flower. The prerequisite for this, however, is that the plants are receiving a minimum amount of light daily. This is a combination of the length of time and the strength of the light, but the exact values have yet to be determined. Also, the question whether the length of the day could have an effect on the flower formation of individual species (photoperiodismus) has apparently not yet been investigated in *Datura*. There are at least quantitative differences between the species with regard to their requirement for light. It has been noticed that *Datura metel*, if given additional lighting in winter, flowers more easily than *D. wrightii* or *D. inoxia*. If there is too little light then the two last-named drop any flowers that are at bud stage before they grow to maturity. *Brugmansia sanguinea* also drops its flower buds prematurely, but the cause is temperatures that are too high.

The transformation of the vegetative sprout tip into a flower, and the sprouting of side shoots that is the result, corresponds to the growth schematic shown for *Brugmansia* (see page 20). The flower at the tip of the shoot on a *Datura* is followed by a forked branching or dichotome much more often than on a *Brugmansia*. Consequently, older *Datura* plants will in general be much broader.

Under natural light conditions in winter, where no flowers are induced, *Datura* as a rule do not branch. Even giving the seedlings support does not improve their plant structure. If you want compact branched seedling plants it is recommended that you do not sow seed before the end of February.

Because *Datura* are short-lived and grown for their summer flowers, they are more often described as annuals. Genuine annuals die off completely after flowering and forming seed — even when conditions are favorable — and they could continue to grow. *Datura* do tend to want to die off if light conditions are poor in winter, but if you protect them from frost they will live for several years.

Thorn Apples are distinctive because of the upright position of their flowers and for two other peculiarities. One refers to the flower corolla. As we know from *Brugmansia*, the flower corolla consists of a tube of five — in exceptions, more than five — flower petals that have grown together. You can recognize the middle of each flower petal from the three flower veins that run longitudinally along it. The middle one of these ends in an elongated peak. *Brugmansia* have only "genuine" peaks that result from a stronger growth of the middle of the flower petal. In many species of *Datura*, small peaks also appear on the stunted seams of the flower petals. These undulations between the flower petals are described as "inter-acuminal peaks".

The second peculiarity applies to the sepals that on *Brugmansia* do not grow after the flower has opened. They either stay in their green state (as on *Brugmansia sanguinea*) until the fruit is ripe or they dry off immediately after the flower is pollinated (as on *B. suaveolens*). On *Datura* the calyx either falls off completely at the beginning of the fruit development or remains like a small ring at the base. As the fruit develops, this ring grows into a conspicuous thick skin (see page 10).

On all *Brugmansia*, the fruit covering is fleshy to floury. It surrounds two seed chambers and when ripe disintegrates irregularly into small pieces. *Datura*, on the other hand, usually has four seed chambers. In some species these are released when the fruit shell falls apart irregularly (*Datura metel*); in others a firm fruit shell forms that opens at the same time the fruit ripens (*Datura stramonium*). The fruit is described as a capsule when it opens at a prescribed breaking point, when the fruit is ripe. Floury, fleshy fruit coverings are classified as berries. The fruits of some *Datura* species, for example *D. wrightii*, fall apart in relatively large pieces and are therefore intermediary forms between berries and capsules. For this reason the term "berry-capsule" was introduced.

The outer nature of the seed is an unmistakable characteristic for distinguishing the two genera: while *Datura* has a simple, rather smooth seed casing, *Brugmansia* seeds are surrounded by an additional cork-like casing that considerably increases the size of the individual seeds. This is doubtless an advantage when distribution is by flowing water. In their native habitats Angel's Trumpets often grow by streams. *Datura* usually grow in drier locations. Some species that have eye-catching whitish attachments known as strophiole or elaiosome on the seed scar (hilum) apparently use ants to help them spread their seeds. The elaiosome consists of nutrient-rich tissue that the plant offers the ant as food. This is why the ants drag the seeds away.

How to classify Thorn Apples

*I*t is not easy to classify a Thorn Apple with certainty. On the one hand, various species such as *D. wrightii* and *D. inoxia* are very similar in appearance. On the other hand, the range of variation within a species can be very broad.

In the chapter on Angel's Trumpets we discussed the problems of classifying plants that have a wide range of variation within each characteristic property. Unfortunately, *Datura* also have the extremely interesting property of being able to change size of plant, size of leaf and size of flowers depending on the location. The same Thorn Apple, when growing in a half-shady, damp location, will develop into a magnificent flowering bush about 3 ft (1 m) tall, but when growing in a very dry location it will only grow into a thin little plant about 4 in (10 cm) high with little flowers and a few miniature leaves.

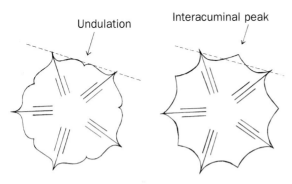

Left: Diagram of a five-peaked flower corolla (*Datura stramonium*). (Corolla five-toothed; the lobes are distinguished by short sinuses.) Right: Diagram of a ten-peaked flower corolla (*Datura leichhardtii*). (Corolla ten-toothed with interacuminal lobules.)

Luckily, *Datura* are able to fertilize themselves and can set fruit with viable seeds on even the tiniest flower. The fruit of the different species of *Datura* has specific behavior patterns. When they ripen, they either fall to pieces or open out, and this property, which is typical of a species, can be used as an alternative way of classifying *Datura*.

In 1983 Hammer, Romeike and Titel worked out such a dichotome key. This key also enables the plant enthusiast to classify the different species with relative certainty. The properties used for classification are explained briefly below and sometimes illustrated.

Characteristics for *Datura* classification

1.	Fruit:	with spines with conical humps bald falls irregularly when ripe; opens regularly when ripe; usually four flaps (see page 113)
2.	Seeds:	color
3.	Flowers:	color double or single size edge with or without interacuminal peaks, i.e. five- or ten-peaked (see diagram opposite)
4.	Leaves and shoots:	furry color leaf shape
5.	Overall plant:	size

Datura fruits compared: regular opening (left and middle); irregularly falling apart (right).

The key below is made up of pairs of mutually exclusive statements. Starting with pair one (1, 1'), work through the key to identify the species. Each statement will have either a species name or will direct you to the next pair of statements. For example, start at 1. If the plant is like a tree with pendulous or nodding flowers it will be a *Brugmansia*. If, however, the plant is only partly woody and has upright flowers, go to statement 2. If the fruits hang down, go to statement 3. If the fruits are bald, you are looking at *D. ceratocaula*. If they are spiny or have conical humps you are directed to statement 4; and so on until a species name is given.

If this statement is true	*Then, go to:*
1 Plants are like trees, flowers pendulous or nodding	*Brugmansia*
1' Plants are weed-like, partly woody flowers are upright	2
2 Fruits hang downwards	3
2' Fruits are upright sec. *Datura*	8
3 Fruits are bald, when ripe fall apart irregularly sec. *Ceratocaulis*	*D. ceratocaula*
3' Fruits are spiny or have conical humps sec. *Datura*	4
4 Fruits open regularly, four flaps	*D. dicolor*
4' Fruits, when ripe, fall apart irregularly; rarely fall as a whole	5
5 Fruits have conical humps	*D. metel*
Flowers are white or yellow	a
Flowers are violet to red (at least partly)	c
a Flowers are simple, white	var *metel*
a' Flowers are double	b
b Flowers are white	var *muricata*
b' Flowers are yellow	var *chlorantha*
c Flowers are single	var *rubra*
violet	f. *rubra*
red	f. *sanguinea*
c' Flowers are double	d
d Flowers are single color, violet or red	var *obscura*
violet	f. *obscura*
red	f. *atropurpurea*
d' Flowers (outer) are violet or red,	
(inner) white	var *fastuosa*
(outer) violet	f. *fastuosa*
(outer) red	f. *malabarica*
5' Fruits usually have sharp piercing spines	6
6 Flowers are relatively small, up to 3 in (7 cm) long, usually few opening	*D. leichhardtii*

Plants are usually taller than 18 in (0.5 m), leaves and shoots are lightly furry	ssp. *leichhardtii*
Plants are not usually taller than 18 in (0.5 m), leaves and shoots are very furry	ssp. *pruinosa*
6' Flowers are relatively large, more than 4 in (10 cm) long	7
7 Interacuminal peak is extremely short, flower edge is evenly rounded, flowers in upper section are usually violet or pale violet seeds are yellowish	*D. wrightii*
7' Interacuminal peak is longer, flower edge is wavy, seeds are medium brown	*D. inoxia*
8 Fruit is either bald or covered with spines, all of which are almost the same length	*D. stramonium*
a Plants are green, flowers are white	b
a' Plants are anthocyan colored, flowers are violet	c
b Fruit is spiny (sometimes bald and spiny fruit on one plant)	var *stramonium*
Fruit is all spiny	f. *stramonium*
Bald and spiny fruit on one plant	f. *labilis*
b' Fruit without spines	var *inermis*
c Fruit spiny	var *tatula*
Anthocyan coloring is less noticeable	f. *tatula*
Anthocyan coloring is very noticeable	f. *bernhardii*
c' Fruit does not have spines	var *godronii*
8' Spines are very strong, longer in upper part of the fruit	9
9 Upper spines are almost as long as the fruit capsule, leaves are toothed irregularly, undulated	*D. ferox*
9' Upper spines are about a third of the length of the fruit, leaves deeply undulated, lobed	*D. quercifolia*

Classification Key
(altered according to Hammer, Romeike and Titel, 1983)
sec. = sectio, section   var = varietas, variety
ssp. = sub-species   f. = forma, form

The wild species of Thorn Apple

Datura ceratocaula Ortega

*T*owards the end of the 18th century a plant was being grown in the Royal Botanical Gardens in Madrid, Spain, that was botanically still unknown. The seed had been gathered in Cuba. In 1797 Ortega named it *Datura ceratocaula* (*ceratocaulus* = stalk like a horn) because of its stem sections that were curved like a horn.

This plant had originally come from Mexico. Centuries earlier the Aztecs called it "Sister of Ololiuqui" (Ololiuqui = *Turbina corymbosa*, a hallucinogen that was frequently used in ritual ceremonies). It was revered as a magic drug and considered to be holy. Before the priest allowed it to be taken for medicinal purposes, he would treat it with great respect, pray to it and ask for its help. Even in more recent times, the many Indian tribes in Central and South America knew of the strong intoxicating properties of *D. cerotocaula* and they used it freely. Nowadays the colloquial name for *D. ceratocaula*, "Torna Loco" (plant that makes you crazy), is a reminder of the strong effect of its contents.

In its natural habitat the weedy *D. ceratocaula* grows in shallow water or in a swamp. Its hollow, gray-green mature stalk is between 12–36 in (30–90 cm) long. It bears ovate-lanceolate leaves that are undulated and toothed and have short white hairs on the underside.

The large, sweet-scented flowers appear from June to September. These are broad and funnel-shaped. Their inner sides are colored white to violet-pink and their outer sides have a bluish coloring. As in all species of *Datura* that have interacuminal peaks, the flower edge of *D. ceratocaula* has ten peaks. The flowers open at midday and close on the following morning.

After successful pollination, the pendulous, completely smooth fruit capsules develop. They look like inverted eggs. As they ripen, they fall apart irregularly and release between 150 to 250 seeds per fruit. The seed is gray-black in color, shiny, with a conspicuous elaiosome. Its mass of a

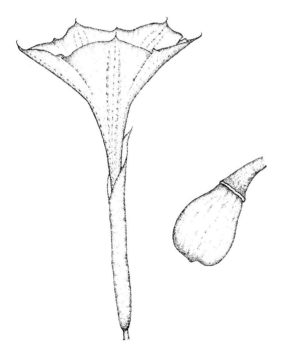

Datura ceratocaula: flower and fruit.

Datura ceratocaula in its natural habitat near Queretaro, Mexico. (Photo: Dr Jöns.) Left: The flowers of *Datura ceratocaula* reach a size of 7 in (18 cm).

being cultivated. A major prerequisite for producing flowers is a sunny, warm location outside. Thanks to their tolerance of damp soil, these plants lend themselves to all kinds of arrangements. Group plantings consisting of several individual examples along the banks of ponds or in damp zones are particularly beautiful. You should take precautions, however, in case domestic or wild animals can regularly cross the land and graze. Otherwise, the result could be what happened in the case described by Reko (1949):

"A species of wild duck lives in the lagoons and swamps near Mazatlan (Mexico). Their meat is said to be poisonous at certain times and eating these ducks has often produced strange symptoms of having been drugged or poisoned. For a long time it was believed that this was somehow connected with the sexual maturity of these animals. Then it was discovered that it was a daturine poisoning. These ducks like to eat the leaves and seeds of the toloachi (*Datura* spec.) and in autumn their flesh contains a percentage of daturine which is very dangerous for people."

thousand seeds weighs approximately $^1/_5$–$^1/_4$ oz (6.5–8 g).

Compared to other species of *Datura*, the plants have only a slight tendency to fork. Their growth is consequently rather sparse but *D. ceratocaula* is still one of the species most worthy of

115

Datura discolor

Datura discolor Bernhardi

In 1833 J. J. Bernhardi in his paper "On the Species of the Genus Datura" described *Datura discolor* for the first time. In this species the term "discolor" (various colors) refers to the interesting color of the individual flowers. The upper section is white, in the center they have a ring-shaped, pale to dark violet coloring.

D. *discolor* is shrubby, either upright or low-lying and grows up to a maximum height of 4$^1/_2$ ft (1.5 m). Its stalks are conspicuously streaked with violet while the foliage is light green. The ovate-shaped leaves are either whole or are toothed with occasional large dentations.

With an average length of the flowers of 5$^1/_2$–6$^1/_2$ in (14–16 cm), and occasionally up to 6$^1/_2$ in (17 cm), D. *discolor* is one of the species of *Datura* that has the largest flowers. It is therefore

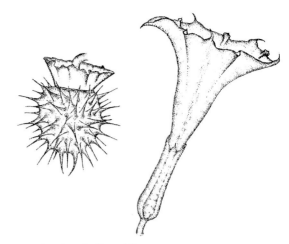

Datura discolor: fruit and flower.

fully worthy of being cultivated in a garden even though each individual flower remains open for only one night and dies during the morning hours of the following day. The slightly wavy flower edge has ten peaks. All five interacuminal peaks are shaped like broad triangles.

After successful pollination, the ovate fruit capsule is formed. It is pendulous and grows to a maximum of 2$^1/_2$–3 in (6–7 cm) in length. It is 2–2$^1/_2$ in (4–6 cm) wide and is covered with long, thin spines. During the ripening period, the base of the calyx broadens into a small disc that, like a cuff, separates fruit and fruit stalk from each other.

Towards the end of the ripening period, the fruit casing breaks evenly into four segments and releases the black seeds with their white elaiosome. Each fruit capsule produces between 250 and 350 seeds; its total mass of a thousand seeds weighs up to $^1/_2$ oz (8–10 g).

The natural distribution area of this heat-loving species of *Datura* stretches from Mexico to the southwestern parts of the U.S.A. and the Caribbean Islands. D. *discolor* prefers a warm, dry, sunny position in the garden as well. Its flowers are erect and it does particularly well in beds underneath overhanging eaves, as this protects the flowers from too much rain.

Datura ferox Linnaeus

Datura ferox was first described in 1756 by Linnaeus. The species description *ferox* means "strongly fortified" and alludes to the spines on the fruit capsule that are particularly fearsome. These distinguish it clearly from the other species of *Datura*.

This *Datura* is more interesting than decorative. It most likely originated in southeastern China, but it was introduced into Europe very early on. Today it can be found in all the warmer regions of the earth and is feared as a dangerous pasture weed.

Datura ferox grows upright into a shrub up to a height of 1½–3 ft (0.5–1 m). The thick stalks are predominantly green but frequently have a reddish violet coloring at the base. It is interesting that the stalks of seedlings are colored an intense violet and only become green above the cotyledon. All the young shoots are noticeably furry. The most conspicuous part of the plant is undoubtedly the very wide foliage leaves that are undulate and irregularly toothed. They are covered with numerous soft hairs that make it look downy.

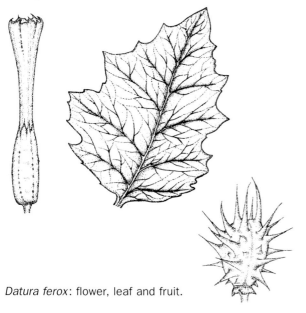

Datura ferox: flower, leaf and fruit.

The rather insignificant, funnel-shaped flowers grow to 2–2½ in (4.5–6 cm) in length and are colored yellowish white. They have five short peaks, no interacuminal peaks and usually do not open completely.

After pollination the fruit capsule develops in an erect position. It is shaped like an inverted egg. During the ripening period the base of the calyx broadens into a disc with a slightly turned down edge. The fruit reaches a maximum size of about 2 in (5–6 cm) in length and 1½ in (4–5 cm) in width. It is well protected by its fearsome spines that grow to ½–1½ in (1.5–3.5 cm) in length. In individual cases the longest spine, which is found at the tip of the fruit, can be as long as the fruit capsule itself. The capsule opens evenly so that all four flaps can release seed. Each capsule contains between 150 and 400 black seeds. Their total mass of a thousand seeds weighs a little over ½ oz (14–16 g).

There is not much value in cultivating *D. ferox*, but, if you are really interested in this genus of plants then you should include this species in your collection mainly because of its interesting leaves.

Datura inoxia Miller
syn. *Datura meteloides*

Datura inoxia was first described in 1768 by the English gardener and botanist Philip Miller. His *D. inoxia* had a white flower corolla that was 6–7 in (15–18 cm) long, grew upright to 7 ft (2 m) and bore fruit with long, sharp spines. Since then plants have been found under this species description whose properties differ from the original description in some details. This includes some plants that used to be called *D. meteloides*. The name *D. meteloides* has since been dropped. It caused numerous *Datura* enthusiasts a lot of uneasiness; the species name "meteloides" alludes to a close kinship with *D. metel* that clearly does not exist. Dunal used this name because of a mistake. In 1852 he described his *D. meteloides* from a picture of a plant provided by Mociño and Sessé. The plants were subtitled *D. metel* but apparently portrayed *D. inoxia* or *D. wrightii*.

D. inoxia originally came from Central and South America. The Aztecs had a highly developed civilization and they used the plant medicinally and as a hallucinogen. At an early stage the plant reached Africa and Asia where it was soon growing wild in the warmer regions.

D. inoxia grows upright into a shrub about 1¹⁄₂–7 ft (0.5–2 m) in height. The young shoots of the green plants are covered thickly with numerous glandular hairs that become fewer on older sections. The soft leaves are a broad oval shape. The leaf edges are whole, but occasionally undulate and toothed in the lower section.

Like *D. wrightii*, *D. inoxia* forms perennial rhizomes. In colder regions these should be kept over winter in the cellar where there is no danger

Datura inoxia

of frost. At the beginning of May the following year, the fragile rootstock can be planted out in the garden again. They do need more time to grow and to form new shoots than young plants grown from seed. By the time they flower though, this disadvantage will have been evened out by faster growth, thanks to the reserves in the rootstocks.

The flowers are about 4 in (9 cm) across and shaped like a funnel. They are 4¹⁄₂–7¹⁄₂ in (12–19 cm) long, and pure white in color. The greenish veins end in five longer peaks. The interacuminal peaks that lie between are noticeably wider and longer than on *D. wrightii*.

After pollination the fruit capsule develops. It is pendulous and its surface is covered with fine hairs and thin, sharp spines. The fruit on a type found in Cuba is covered with large, roundish humps like *D. metel*. This is why, in 1980, Fuentes published it as a new species, *Datura velutinosa*. Because the new *D. velutinosa* was

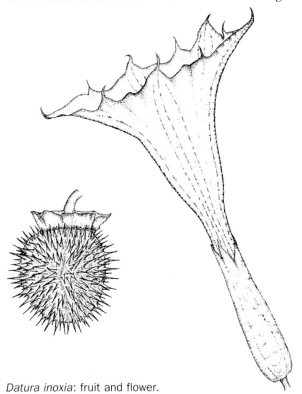

Datura inoxia: fruit and flower.

similar in all other ways to *D. inoxia*, it did not find overall acceptance. Usually it is classified together with other forms of *D. inoxia*.

As in many species of *Datura*, the base of the calyx falls off and the base that remains broadens into a wide disc. Once the fruit has reached its final size of about 2–3 in (5–7 cm), then it falls apart irregularly and releases between 350 to 500 seeds. The medium brown seeds are usually slightly darker than those of *D. wrightii*. When they are ready for harvesting, they carry an elaisome. The mass of a thousand seeds weighs more than ¹/₂ oz (12–17 g).

D. inoxia, with its large radiant white flowers, is one of the most beautiful species of *Datura*. Like all Thorn Apples it prefers a sunny location where overhanging eaves or large trees keep most of the rain off its magnificent flowers.

The flowers of *Datura leichhardtii* ssp. *pruinosa* frequently do not open. Below: fruit and flower of *Datura leichhardtii*.

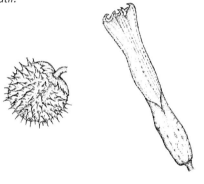

Datura leichhardtii
F. v. Müeller

In 1844 Leichhardt is said to have discovered this species by the Comet River in northern Queensland, Australia. The German-Australian botanist Sir Ferdinand Jacob Heinrich von Müller, therefore, gave it the name *Datura leichhardtii* when he published his first description in 1855. Its preferred habitat is close to watercourses, and today it is widely spread throughout Australia.

The natural habitat of this species stretched from Mexico to Guatemala. It was taken to Australia, where we now distinguish between two sub-species: *Datura leichhardtii* ssp. *leichhardtii* and *Datura leichhardtii* ssp. *pruinosa*. There is not a lot of difference between them. Hammer et al. (1983) explained the similarity of the characteristics by the fact that the period of isolation of the two sub-species is still relatively short. Thus, *Datura leichhardtii* ssp. *leichhardtii* is found mainly in the half-arid regions of Queensland,

central Australia, and in the northwest of Western Australia, but not in northwestern New South Wales or southwestern Queensland, even though the climates are comparable. The geographical separation promises that in the future the two sub-species will develop independently and that possibly they will develop specific typical characteristics that will distinguish them.

The annual *D. leichhardtii* grows upright into a bush. *Datura leichhardtii* ssp. *leichhardtii* attains the stately height of 3–4 ft (1–1.2 m), but *Datura leichhardtii* ssp. *pruinosa* remains relatively small with a maximum height of only 18 in

(0.5 cm). The plants are green and slightly furry. *D.l.* ssp. *pruinosa* is slightly furrier. The rather inconspicuous, yellowish white flower corolla is only 1¹/₂–2 in (4–7 cm) long. It is ten-peaked, as it has slight interacuminal peaks. Occasionally, the flower edge has a hint of a light green or reddish tone.

The fruit capsule develops after successful pollination. It is pendulous, round, covered in short spines and barely 1¹/₂ in (4 cm) in diameter. During the ripening period, the calyx falls off and the base, which remains, broadens into a wide disc with down-turned rim that wraps around the capsule like a narrow cuff.

Towards the end of the ripening period, the fruit falls apart irregularly and releases between 25 and 100 brown seeds to which starch-rich pieces of tissue (elaiosomes) are attached. Its mass of a thousand seeds weighs about ¹/₂ oz (14–16 g).

D. leichhardtii is extremely fond of heat. It is not found in cultivation, as its small inconspicuous flowers have no ornamental value. Moreover, they do not open completely.

Datura metel Linnaeus

Because *Datura metel* is widely used by people both as a drug and an ornamental plant, it is grown all over the world. It can also be found growing in the wild in all the warmer regions. It is now impossible to be certain where its original homeland was.

When Linnaeus wrote his first description in 1753 he stated that *Datura metel* came from Asia and Africa. He gave it the species descriptive name of "metel" and equated it with the plant described by the Arab doctor and scholar Avicenna in the 11th century as "jouz-mathel", i.e. metel nut, because of its fruits. It remains unknown whether Avicenna's jouz-mathel is identical to Linnaeus's *Datura metel*. The first unmistakable

Datura metel: fruit and flower.

picture of a *Datura metel* was not published until 1543 when the German Leonhard Fuchs included it in his now famous "Book of Herbs". Like his predecessors, Leonhard Fuchs included a very imprecise description with his drawing. The drawing was apparently copied from a medical book "De Materia Medica" by the Greek Dioscorides that appeared in the first century. Even in ancient Chinese literature *Datura metel* cannot be proven to exist until the year 1658. Li Shi Chen described it at that time as *Datura alba*.

It seems no illustrations or descriptions that are botanically correct were made until after Europeans landed in America. David E. Symon et al. (1991) assume, therefore, that any mention of earlier references in literature are based on mistakes and that the origin of *Datura metel* is to be found in the New World. This means that *Datura metel* was one of the first species of plant that, in the decades after the European colonization of America, was spread worldwide by people —

Opposite: *Datura metel* var *fastuosa*

Above: *Datura metel* var *chlorantha*. Right: This single form of *Datura metel* var *rubra* is only colored violet on the outer side of the flower corolla.

even without tourism *en masse*. This species of *Datura* was apparently much in demand because of its narcotic effect. The fact that its seeds propagate easily also helped it to spread.

Datura metel is an annual herb and reaches its mature size of 1½–3 ft (0.5–1 m) after a few months. The plants are slightly furry and the shoots are usually dark violet in color. The oval to broad oval, undulate or coarsely toothed leaves often have the same coloring.

The flowers, which are immensely varied, are without doubt its most conspicuous and most interesting characteristic. During the day they emit a pleasant scent. According to variety and shape they can be single or double, five to nine peaks and can be colored pure white, cream, yellow, red or violet. Danert (1954) differentiated between 11 different groups.

D. metel has conspicuous, heart-shaped cuts in place of the interacuminal peaks. These make decorative dividers on the large flowers that are 6–8 in (14–20 cm) in size.

The upright, ovate- to round-shaped fruit capsule develops after successful pollination. Its surface is lightly furry and is covered with numerous conical humps and a few spines. After the ripening period, the capsule falls apart irregularly and releases between 200 and 300 seeds. They are colored dark to brownish yellow and have a conspicuous elaiosome. The mass of a thousand seeds weighs nearly 1 oz (15–20 g).

Of all the species of *Datura*, *D. metel* is undoubtedly the species most frequently cultivated in gardens. Its large, funnel-shaped flowers come in a wealth of colors and shapes. To differentiate them clearly from Angel's Trumpets, *D. metel* was called "Devil's Trumpet" in the southern states of the U.S.A.

Unfortunately, the devil's trumpet is very susceptible to an inflammation of the roots that can be caused by all kinds of harmful fungi, particularly in years when the summer months are damp and rainy. If possible it should be planted in dry locations in the garden, preferably under overhanging eaves.

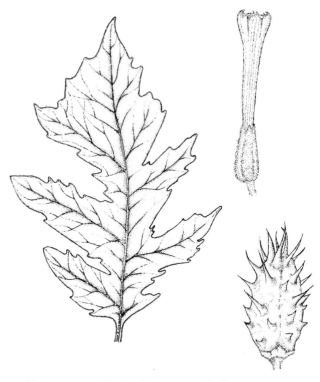

Datura quercifolia: leaf, flower and fruit.

Datura quercifolia Humboldt

The first description of *Datura quercifolia* was made in 1818 by Friedrich Wilhelm Heinrich Alexander von Humboldt. The species classification "quercifolia" is a very apt description of the leaves of this species that are oak-shaped.

Datura quercifolia comes from Mexico and the southwestern states of the U.S.A. There it grows as a ground cover or into an upright bush up to a height of 1¹/₂–3 ft (0.5–1 m). The green shoots of the plants frequently have a pale violet coloring on the base. The oak-like foliage leaves are undulate to deeply undulate and lobed. Their

Right: *Datura quercifolia* has small blue flowers and an unmistakable leaf shape.

123

leaf edge is slightly wavy. The veins on the underside of the leaf are very furry.

In contrast to the decoratively shaped leaves, the flowers are unremarkable. They are only 1¹/₂–2 in (4–7 cm) long and funnel-shaped. In addition, the flower corollas usually do not open fully and, therefore, their light blue flowers are hardly shown to advantage. The flower edge has five short peaks. There are no interacuminal peaks.

The ovate, upright fruit capsule develops after successful pollination, which can take place while the flower is still closed, from its own flower pollen. It becomes 2¹/₂ in (7 cm) long and 2 in (6 cm) wide and has sharp spines that can be up to a third the length of the capsule. During the ripening period, the base of the calyx broadens to a disc with a turned-down edge. The four flaps of the ripe fruit capsule open evenly and release between 250 to 400 seeds per capsule. The seeds are black. Their mass of a thousand seeds weighs up to ¹/₂ oz (7–10 g).

Because of its tiny insignificant flowers, *D. quercifolia* does not have much ornamental value. If you are making a collection of different *Daturas*, though, you should include this species because of the interesting shape of its leaves and decorative fruit.

Datura stramonium Linnaeus

In 1753 Linnaeus described *Datura stramonium* for the first time. This plant, however, had caused a sensation 80 years earlier:

In 1676 British soldiers in North America were commanded to go to Jamestown to suppress a rebellion. They were acutely short of food and, out of ignorance or through a misunderstanding, they cooked up the young shoots and leaves of *Datura stramonium* and ate them as a vegetable. After a while they showed strange changes in their behavior. They fell into a type of trance or "com-

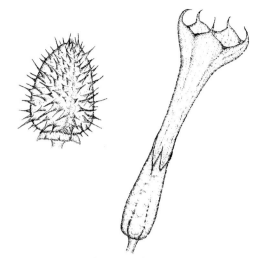

Datura stramonium: fruit and flower.

ical madness" that made them have all sorts of foolish notions and act stupidly. One of them tried again and again to make a feather climb in the air and another threw straw until he was completely exhausted. A third sat stark naked in a corner and contorted his face like an ape into a continual grin. Everything they did was totally non-violent; they were simply good-naturedly idiotic. The effects of *Datura stramonium* lasted for a full eleven days (Safford, 1920). Not until then was the last of the drugged soldiers himself again. It is interesting that they could not remember anything. Since those days, the colloquial name for *Datura stramonium* in North America has been "Jamestown weed", which over time became "Jimson weed".

The Indians had known about *Datura stramonium* for centuries. They knew its hallucinogenic effect and used the drug in many of their ceremonies.

Originally, *D. stramonium* came from the southeast of North America. People spread it very early on. Nowadays, it grows wild in all the moderate and warm regions of the world. Even in Europe this annual weed prefers to grow on wasteland and around garbage dumps.

Datura stramonium grows upright into a bush up to 7 ft (0.2–2 m) high. The green plants

Datura stramonium var *tatula* f. *tatula* with violet coloring in the center of the flower corolla.

frequently look as though they are covered with a thin violet layer and their younger shoots are delicately furry. The soft foliage leaves are irregularly undulate and toothed. One of the most noticeable and less pleasant characteristics of this plant is its pungent, nut-like smell that becomes stronger even if it is only lightly touched.

The flowers are funnel-shaped. They are 2½–3½ in (6–8.5 cm) long, have just five sharp peaks, and no interacuminal peaks. Their flowers are white- to creamy-colored or violet. The ornamental value of the flowers is not great as they very rarely open completely.

After pollination the ovate, upright fruit capsule develops. Its surface can be covered with spines or it can be totally bald. During the ripening period the base of the calyx broadens into a flat disc. After the fruit has reached its final size of a maximum of 1½ in (4 cm) in length and 1 in (3 cm) in width, the four flaps of the capsule open and each releases between 300 and 500 seeds. The seed is black and a mass of a thousand seeds weighs about ½ oz (7–11 g).

Because of its appearance, *D. stramonium* is not worth cultivating. If you would still like to have this species of plant, then you should keep a watchful eye on the development of the fruit capsule and remove it if necessary at the right time. If the seed falls out uncontrollably, then the following year you will have *Datura* seedlings throughout the whole garden.

Datura wrightii Regel

In 1855 a new *Datura* under the name *Datura meteloides* was cultivated in the garden of the famous French nursery of Louis Vilmorin. The botanist Asa Gray, who was working at Harvard University, sent the seeds to France. Gray himself got the seeds from the North American plant collector Charles Wright who had gathered them in 1849 in western Texas. M. Ortgies, a colleague in Vilmorin's nursery, noticed that the *Datura* they had cultivated did not agree with the description

Left and opposite: *Datura wrightii* has the largest flowers of all the species of *Datura*.

the scientific description of a new species of *Datura* with pale violet flower corollas. In acknowledgment of its discoverer, he named it *Datura wrightii*.

The original homeland of *D. wrightii* is southern North America and the whole of Mexico. Because of its beauty and its hallucinogenic contents, very early on it was taken to the warmer regions of the rest of the world, including Australia, where it now grows wild.

D. wrightii grows into a bush either upright or low-lying up to a height of 5 ft (0.4–1.5 m). The green shoots of the plant often look as if they are covered with a thin violet layer. All the young leaves are noticeably furry but they become less so as they age. The soft leaves are ovate to broadly ovate. The edge of the leaf is coarsely toothed or gently undulate. *D. wrightii* forms a tuberous, fleshy rootstock that enables the plant to over-winter in the ground where the locations are not too cold. It then puts out shoots the following spring. In colder regions the rootstock can be over-wintered in the cellar, like dahlia bulbs.

The funnel-shaped flower corollas are 5–9 in (14–23 cm) long and attain a diameter of 5 in (15 cm). The upper section is usually violet to pale violet. Pure white examples are rare. The flowers are very decorative. They have five clearly defined peaks that are about ¼ in (0.5 cm) long. In between you can often find sets of interacuminal peaks, which is why some authors describe the flower corolla of *Datura wrightii* as ten-peaked.

The fruit capsule develops after successful pollination. It is pendulous, covered with blunt spines and fine hairs. Like many other species it also has a small collar cuff that develops from the residue of the calyx and then broadens out. The berry capsule is nearly 2 in (4.5 cm) in size. On ripening it falls apart irregularly and releases 200

of *Datura meteloides* that Felix Dunal had published in 1852. Ortgies informed the German botanist Eduard August von Regel, who published the journal "Gartenflora", of this discrepancy. As a consequence, in 1859 Regel published

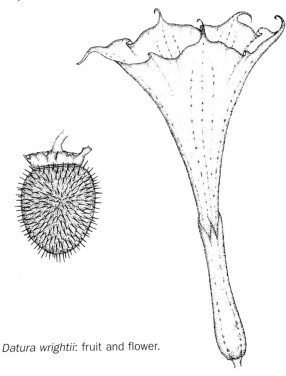

Datura wrightii: fruit and flower.

to 400 seeds. The seed is yellowish brown. Its mass of a thousand seeds weighs more than $\frac{1}{2}$ oz (14–16 g).

D. *wrightii* has large flowers and is well worth cultivating. Its full beauty can be seen either planted out as a bedding plant or in a tub as a container plant. As the large flower corollas point upwards they quickly fill with water. Plants should be planted out either under overhanging eaves or where they are protected from the rain. This prevents the white flowers from going brown or being stuck together, which is unsightly.

Are there other species?

*I*t often happens that new descriptions of species are accepted prematurely. Later it becomes apparent that these new species are simply varieties that have evolved as reactions to conditions at a specific location. Daturas self-pollinate and easily produce variations when they settle on wasteland. After a few years, as shrubs and trees repopulate the area, or as a result of other factors caused by the environment, these new forms usually disappear. There are often several classifications in use for the same species within the species *Datura*. These are considered to be invalid according to the rules of nomenclature, but can be viewed as synonyms.

In some cases insufficient information, mistakes and confusion mean that it is impossible to know what the original plant being described actually looked like. You can understand why if you consider that *Datura* have been spread by the migrations of people since time immemorial and that the botanical nomenclature, which is still valid today, was founded by Linnaeus as early as 1753.

The following is a list of names of species which should probably be regarded as synonyms of the species of *Datura* described in the previous chapter.

Note: (?) after an entry indicates that the classification is uncertain. Due to loss of herbarium specimens and incomplete descriptions by the authors, the exact identification is not always possible.

Datura alba Nees, 1834 = *Datura metel* var *metel*

Datura bernhardii Lundström, 1914 = *Datura stramonium* var *tatula* f. *bernhardii*

Datura bertolonii Parlatore ex Gussone, 1842 = *Datura stramonium* var *inermis*

Datura bojeri Raffeneau-Delile, 1836 = *Datura metel* (?)

Datura capensis hort. ex Bernhardi, 1833 = *Datura stramonium*

Datura carthaginensis hort. ex Siebert et Voss, 1895 = *Datura metel*

Datura cornucopaea hort. ex W. W., 1894 = *Datura metel*

Datura dubia Persoon, 1805 = *Datura metel*
This species is said, however, to have smooth fruit.

Datura fastuosa Linnaeus, 1759 = *Datura metel*

Datura fruticosa Hornem., 1813 = *Datura metel* (?)

Datura guayaquilensis Humboldt, 1818 = *Datura inoxia*

Datura huberiana hort., 1891 = *Datura metel* (?)

Datura humilis Desfontaines, 1829 = *Datura metel*

Datura hummatu Bernhardi, 1833 = *Datura metel*

Datura hybrida Tenore, 1823 = *Datura inoxia* or *D. wrightii*

Datura inermis Jaq., 1776 = *Datura stramonium* var *inermis*

Datura kymatocarpa Barcley, 1959 = *Datura discolor* (?)

Datura laevis Linnaeus, 1781 = *Datura stramonium*

Datura lanosa Barcley ex Bye, 1986 = *Datura wrightii* or *Datura inoxia*

Barcley published this species as a sub-species of *Datura inoxia*. Bye put it in the circle of *Datura wrightii*. In contrast to the former it is said to have a thick felt of long tangled fur on the undersides of the leaves.

Datura loricata Sieber ex Bernhardi, 1833 = *Datura stramonium*

Datura lurida Salisbury, 1796 = *Datura stramonium*

Datura macrocaulos Roth, 1802 = *Datura ceratocaula*

Datura meteloides Dunal, 1852 = *Datura inoxia*

Datura microcarpa Godron, 1872 = *Datura stramonium*

Datura muricata Bernhardi, 1818 = *Datura metel* var *muricata*

Datura nigra Rumph. ex Hassk., 1842 = *Datura metel* var *metel*

Datura nilhummatu Dunal, 1852 = *Datura metel* var *obscura*

Datura parviflora Salisbury, 1796 = *Datura stramonium* var *tatula*

Datura praecox Godron, 1872 = *Datura stramonium* var *tatula*

Datura pruinosa Greenman, 1898 = *Datura leichhardtii* ssp. *pruinosa*

Datura pseudo-stramonium Sieber ex Bernhardi, 1833 = *Datura stramonium*

Datura pubescens Roques, 1808 = *Datura metel* or *D. inoxia*

Datura reburra Barcley, 1959 = *Datura discolor*

Datura sinuata Sessé et Mociño, 1893 = *Datura ceratocaula*

Datura tatula Linnaeus, 1762 = *Datura stramonium* var *tatula*

Datura thomasii Torrey, 1857 = *Datura discolor* (?)

Datura timorensis Zipp. ex Spanoghe, 1841 = *Datura metel* (?)

Datura velutinosa Fuentes, 1980 = *Datura inoxia* (?)

Datura villosa Fernald., 1900 = *Datura quercifolia*

Datura wallichii Dunal, 1852 = *Datura stramonium*

Cultivation

Most of the annual Thorn Apples are suited both to being planted out in beds and being cultivated in containers. They do not require any special treatment in containers other than adequate drainage.

Potting mix

Datura are rather more demanding as regards potting mix. It must be porous and aerated, as *Datura* are very susceptible to harmful fungi in the root area. Avoid adding additional organic enrichers such as humus, peat, compost or stable manure. A high proportion of loam or clay can also be harmful. These increase the water storage capacity, making the work of the damp-loving, harmful fungi easier by helping them to attack in the root area. Inorganic material, such as pumice, scoria or similar material, on the other hand, has a positive effect. These loosen up the mix, let the water drain out faster and increase the air flow to the root area.

When cultivating *D. metel*, which is particularly sensitive, you should add a dosage of a soil fungicide such as Fonganil. This will make cultivation much easier. Add the fungicide to the watering water and water at regular intervals as prescribed in the instructions for use.

D. ceratocaula is the only species of *Datura* that has no problems with soil that contains clay or with having occasional wet feet; as a genuine swamp plant, its roots are well-adjusted to having too much water. All the other species are at home in dry, often desert-like locations. Remember this when watering the plants. You should accustom this genus of plants to frugal watering and try to avoid wetting the delicate flowers. Even after periods of high humidity when the leaves of *Datura* seem to be wilting, test the dampness of the soil first before watering. You will be rewarded by healthy roots and stable plant growth.

Location and watering

*Datura*s have opposite needs to *Brugmansia* and should never be given shower baths. The upright position of the flowers means that the corollas, which open skywards, quickly fill with water. As there is nowhere within the flowers for the water to drain off, the corolla bends at its weakest point to get rid of the burden of the water. The result is unsightly gumming together and flowers that turn brown as they rot. The large-flowered *Datura*s, which open wide, are the worst hit.

Unfortunately, this problem also occurs under continual or heavy rain. You should therefore take this into consideration when looking for a suitable location. All sunny locations are optimal if they are protected from direct rain by over-

Opposite: *Datura wrightii* is suitable for planting out in summer in containers.

hanging eaves or high neighboring plants. Thorn Apples will develop into magnificent plants in such locations where other summer flowers find it too dry.

An optimal location protects the plant from the rain.

Fertilization

Datura have no problems as regards fertilization. During the short summer growth period, they must put on a relatively large amount of leaves and flowers. Every week from May to August, they should be provided with ¹/₂ teaspoon (2–3 g or 2–3 mL) of a complete fertilizer, which includes plenty of nitrogen, per 1¹/₂ pints (1 liter) of water.

When they are being cultivated in beds, you can use a slow-release fertilizer to reduce your workload. According to the degree of effectiveness of the product, you should apply a dose of approximately 2 oz (60 g) of slow-release, high-nitrogen fertilizer per square yard (m²), two to three times during the summer months. Never give organic fertilizers, such as stable manure, guano or compost, because of the plant's susceptibility to harmful fungi.

It is better to avoid giving *Datura* organic fertilizers.

Over-wintering

Thorn Apples are usually cultivated annually. During the summer, you harvest the seeds from the fruit capsules. New plants will be produced from the beginning of March. The mother plants usually die off as the temperatures become colder in winter, though *Datura wrightii* and *Datura inoxia* are exceptions. During the summer months, these two produce thick, fleshy storage roots that allow them to over-winter. In a warm, wine-growing climate, for example, all that is necessary is to cover the plants in the fall with all kinds of twigs, straw or pine needles. Depending on the weather, the *Datura* wake up from their winter sleep from April onwards. In colder climates, the rhizomes must be over-wintered in a container with earth and kept free from frost. Covering with earth prevents the roots from drying out. They can be over-wintered in a cool garage or in dark cellars. From March you should subject the rhizomes to daylight and temperatures of 53°–64°F (12°–18°C) to encourage them to put out growths above the soil. It is more work over-wintering *Datura* than sowing seed annually, but the result is worth the trouble. Plants that sprout from healthy rhizomes develop faster, become bigger, and flower better.

Propagation

The herb Thorn Apples are propagated solely from seed. As many species of *Datura* tend to self-pollinate, the seeds are usually exactly like the mother plant. This property, described as auto-gamy, is particularly predominant among the small-flowered *Datura*. These include *D. stramonium*, *D. ferox*, *D. quercifolia* and *D. leichhardtii*. Pollination has often already taken place before the flower has opened. Danert (1954) found in his research on *D. stramonium* that the anther of this species opens 24 hours before the flower corolla unfolds. This considerably reduces the chance of pollination by a foreign agent. Growers of *Daturas* can harvest seed that is pure to the species from their small-flowered *Datura* if they plant these species together in one bed. They will have to take more care with the large-flowered "beautiful" species of *Datura*, such as *D. ceratocaula, D. wrightii* and *D. inoxia*. These Thorn Apples, if they are isolated from all the other *Datura* plants, will set fruit with viable seeds, but the percentage of fruit that does not develop is above average (Hammer et al. 1983).

In general it can be said that the tendency to be pollinated by a foreign agent increases with the size of the flower corolla. The gleaming white color of the flowers is important as it reflects light. Size of flower and color of flower attract insects to a considerable degree. These will then pollinate the flowers.

Growers of *Daturas* must plant the large-flowered species separate from one another if they want to obtain seeds that are true to the species.

Harvesting the seed can be a nuisance, as ripe fruits burst open and scatter their seed over wide areas. It is recommended, therefore, that the fruit is cut off shortly before it ripens, and if necessary allowed to ripen in a paper bag. The harvesting of a larger number of seeds can stretch over a lengthy period of time from late summer to fall.

In the following March the seeds are sown in a protected greenhouse or on a windowsill at temperatures around 68°F (20°C).

In most species the tiny plants will germinate after 15 to 20 days. Only *D. ceratocaula, D. discolor* and *D. quercifolia* germinate irregularly over a period of up to three months. This annoying hesitancy can be avoided by pre-treating the seeds with 0.2 percent gibberellic acid. The seeds are placed for two days in the weak acid and then sown in the soil.

This treatment replaces a natural effect of cold during the winter months and accelerates the germination of the seeds. After two days' treatment with acid at 71°F (22°C), *D. ceratocaula* and *D. quercifolia* will germinate in four to five days. Even after treatment with gibberellic acid, *D. discolor* will still need 19 to 20 days until the first seed begins to germinate.

The young plants are pricked into small containers and planted out in their final positions at the end of May or when all danger of frost is past.

Breeding

If you are collecting plants of a special genus, then after a while the question arises: Would it be possible to combine the particularly good properties of one species with those of another? How well, for example, would the pleasant scent of plant A harmonize with the wonderful color of plant B? Once you have started asking yourself such questions then the path to breeding them yourself is very short.

Probably the most extensive investigations on *Datura* were carried out by A. F. Blackeslee et al. Their results are published in the standard work on *Datura* "The Genus *Datura*" by Avery et al. (1959) and form the basis for the table below on possible crossbreedings. Many of the combinations between the various species of *Datura* are successful only if specific species are used as the mother plants. Other species are better suited as pollen givers. The following table provides the information on which crossbreedings the garden enthusiast can carry out successfully without using laboratory equipment.

There is a multitude of possible crossbreedings among the species of *Datura*, but you will find

Crossbreedings that have produced seeds capable of germinating

Female \ Male	D. stramonium	D. quercifolia	D. ferox	D. leichhardtii	D. discolor	D. ceratocaula	D. wrightii	D. metel	D. inoxia
D. stramonium	x	x	x		x				
D. quercifolia	x	x	x		x		(x)		
D. ferox	x	x	x		x				
D. leichhardtii	x	x	x	x	x		x		x
D. discolor					x				
D. ceratocaula						x			
D. wrightii							x		
D. metel							(x)	x	(x)
D. inoxia							x		x

(x) = crossbreedings that only occasionally produced seeds capable of germination
Female = mother plant
Male   = pollen giver

only one hybrid form in the wild. This is a cross between *D. stramonium* and *D. ferox* that has been seen in various locations in South America. The fact that the individual species grow in very different areas would explain why only one natural hybrid has been found. The main reason for the purity of the species within this genus is because of its tendency to self-pollinate. To get around this characteristic described as autogamy, the grower of *Datura* must observe some important rules when pollinating plants.

Pollination

Before the flowers open you must remove all five stamens from the mother plant by making a cut through the wall of the flower. You should test whether the stamen is still closed, as only then can you be sure that it has not self-pollinated. Finally, wipe the pollen from the pollen giver onto the stigma of the mother plant. In order to rule out any subsequent pollination, it is recommended that you protect the flower against its environment by wrapping it in a small paper bag.

Obtaining the seed

Since the moment of maturing, and therefore when the fruit will burst open, cannot be calculated to the day, you should wrap the fruit capsules in a paper or fabric bag when they are almost ripe. In this way you prevent the loss of the valuable seed that otherwise would be scattered over a large area once the fruit has burst. An alternative is to harvest the seed capsules just before they ripen and let them ripen in a warm, dry environment until they burst. If you then store the seed somewhere dry and cool it will keep its germination qualities for several years.

As *Datura* fruits often split open uncontrollably and scatter their poisonous seeds, you should never let these plants grow near vegetable or herb beds.

Diseases and pests

Naturally, the *Datura* genus has to fight numerous pests and diseases, though in contrast to *Brugmansia* the deadly virus diseases hardly feature. Thorn Apples benefit from the fact that they can be relatively easily propagated by seed and, as a rule, seed is free from viruses. Should you notice that a *Datura* plant is showing symptoms of a virus (see page 98) during the summer months, then this plant must be removed immediately and destroyed to prevent the virus from spreading.

Piercing-sucking insects like thrips, aphids, whitefly and leaf bugs are responsible for carrying viral infections. *Datura* is unfortunately not exempt. A description of the typical damage they do and the methods for combating them can be found on page 101. The most threatening diseases for *Datura* are root rot, such as root and stalk wilt. These are caused by various fungal agents, such as *Thielaviopsis*, *Phytophtora* or *Pythium*. The beautiful *Datura metel* has unfortunately proven to be particularly susceptible. Leaving the plants standing in wet soil encourages the spread of these diseases. As we can have no effect on the weather in summer, it is recommended that when you plant out you should add soil fungicide. These plant treatment agents are obtainable in specialist shops because they are produced specifically for commercial gardens. If you wait until the typical withering symptoms appear, then you will no longer be able to save the plant. Should the summer prove to be very wet, then it is rec-ommended that you repeat the fungicide treatment at intervals of a few weeks.

Giving the plants optimum growth conditions is better than fighting the diseases as they appear. Strong, healthy plants are best able to resist diseases and pests.

Choosing the correct location is especially important for *Datura*s. It is helpful to orient yourself to the conditions where it grows in its native habitat. As a rule, *Datura*s need warm, sunny places and soil that is not inducive to wet feet. If necessary, improve the aeration of the soil around the roots by mixing in inorganic fillers, such as pumice, scoria or similar material, as this makes it difficult for the dangerous fungal agents to enter the plants.

Bibliography

AVERY, A. G., SATINA, S. and RIETSEMA, J.: *The Genus Datura*. Ronald Press Company, New York, 1959.

BAILEY, L. H. and BAILEY, E. Z.: *Hortus Third*, Macmillan Publishing Company, New York, 1976.

BARCLEY, A. S.: *Studies in the genus Datura (solanaceae). I. Taxonomy of subgenus Datura*. Doctoral dissertation, Harvard Univ., Cambridge, 1959.

BARCLEY, A. S.: "New considerations in an old genus: *Datura*." *Botanical Museum Leaflets*, Harvard Univ. 18(6): 245–272, 1959.

BERNHARDI, J. J.: "Ueber die Arten der Gattung *Datura*", *Neues Journal für Pharmacie*, 26: 118–158, 1833.

BOSSE, J. F. W. (Pub.): *Vollständiges Handbuch der Blumengärtnerei*. Hahn'sche Hofbuchhandlung Hannover: 401–403, 1840.

BRISTOL, M. L.: "Notes on the species of Tree Daturas." *Botanical Museum Leaflets*, Harvard Univ. 21(8): 299–347, 1966.

BRISTOL, M. L.: "Tree *Datura* drugs of the Colombian Sibundoy." *Botanical Museum Leaflets*, Harvard Univ. 22(5): 165–227, 1969.

BRISTOL, M. L., EVANS, W. C. and LAMPARD, J. F.: "The alkaloides of the genus *Datura*, section *Brugmansia* Part. VI. Tree *Datura* Drugs (*Datura* candida cvs.) of the Colombian Sibundoy." *Lloydia* 32: 123–130, 1969.

DANERT, S.: "Ein Beitrag zur Kenntnis der Gattung *Datura L.*" *Feddes Repetitorium* 57(3): 231–242, 1955.

DAVIS, E. WADE: *Schlange und Regen-bogen*. Droemersche Verlagsanstalt Th. Knaur Nachf., München, 1986.

DAVIS, E. WADE: "Solanaceae." *Botanical Museum Leaflets*, Harvard Univ. 29(3): 202–203, 1983.

DEWOLF, G. P.: "Notes on cultivated Solanaceae. 2. *Datura*." *Baileya* 4: 13–23, 1956.

DUNAL, F. L.: "Solanaceae." In: *De Candolle: Prodomus systemantis naturalis regni vegetabilis*. Victoria Masson, Paris, 1852.

ENCKE. F. (Pub.): *Pareys Blumengärtnerei*. P. Parey, Berlin and Hamburg: 490–491, 1958.

ENCKE, F.: "*Datura* im Kübel." *Gartenpraxis* 8: 410–411, 1976.

ENGELHARDT, ROBERT: "*Datura suaveolens* im Garten zu Thelwall Heyes (England)." *Möllers Deutsche Gärtner-Zeitung II*: 117–119, 1898.

FOSBERG, F. R.: "Nomenclatural notes on *Datura L.*" *Taxon* 8(2): 52–57, 1959.

FROHNE, DIETRICH and PFÄNDER, HANS JÜRGEN: *Giftpflanzen*. Wissenschaftliche Verlagsgesellschaft, Stuttgart, 1982.

FUENTES, V.: "*Datura velutinosa*: Una nueva especie de Solanaceae para Cuba." *Revista del Jardin Botanico Nacional Universidad de La Habana* 1, 53–59, 1980.

HAEGI, L.: "Taxonomic Account of *Datura L.* (solanaceae) in Australia with a Note on *Brug-*

mansia Pers." *Australian Journal of Botany* 24: 415–435, 1976.

HAMMER, K.: "Beobachtungen an *Datura meteloides* Dunal." *Kulturpflanze* 23: 131–137, 1975.

HAMMER, K., ROMEIKE, A. and TITEL, C.: "Vorarbeiten zur monographischen Darstellung von Wilpflanzensortimenten: *Datura L.,* sectiones Dutra Bernh., Ceratocaulis Bernh. et Datura." *Kulturpflanze* 31: 13–75, 1983.

HEGI, GUSTAV: *Datura.* In: "Illustrierte Flor von Mittel-Europa." Band V, 4. *Teil:* 2612–2616. Carl Hanser Verlag, München, 1927.

HOOKER: "*Datura* chlorantha; flore pleno." *Curtis's Botanical Magazine* 85: pl.5128, 1859.

HUXLEY, A., GRIFFITHS, M. and LEVY, M. (Publ): *Dictionary of Gardening.* Macmillan Press, London and Stockton Press, New York, 1992.

KAHN, R. P. and BARTELS, R.: "The Colombian *Datura* Virus — A New Virus in the Potato Virus Y Group." *Phytopathology* 58: 587–591, 1968.

KUGLER, H. v.: "Zur Bestäubung grossblumiger *Datura*-Arten." *Flora* 160: 511–517, 1971.

LAGERHEIM, G.: "Eine neue goldgelbe *Brugmansia.*" *Gartenflora* 42; 33–35, 1893.

LAGERHEIM, G.: "Monographie der ecuadorianischen Arten der Gattung *Brugmansia* Pers." *Engler's Botanische Jahrbücher* 20: 655–668, 1895.

LEMAIRE, CH. (Pub.): *Jardin Fleuriste.* Editeurs F. et E. Gyselynck: 16, 1854.

LOCKWOOD, T. E.: *A taxonomic revision of Brugmansia (solanaceae).* Dissertation Cambridge, Massachusetts, 1973.

LOCKWOOD, T. E.: "Generic recognition of *Brugmansia.*" *Botanical Museum Leaflets,* Harvard Univ. 23 (6): 273–284, 1973.

LOCKWOOD, T. E.: "The ethnobotany of *Brugmansia. J.*" *Ethnopharmacol.* 1: 147–164, 1979.

MENNINGER, E. A.: "*Datura* species in Florida gardens." *Amercian Horticultural Magazine.* 45: 375–387, 1966.

NOTHDURFT, H.: "Die Merkmale der Engelstrompeten." *Gartenpraxis* 6: 270–273, 1979.

PAECH, K.: *Biochemie und Physiologie der sekundären Pflanzenstoffe.* Springer-Verlag, Berlin, Göttingen, Heidelberg, 1950.

PERSOON, C. H.: "Synopsis plantarum sen enchiridium botanicum, complectens numerationem systematicam specierum huscusque cognitarum." *Vol. 1. Parisiss Lutetiorum:* 216–217, 1805.

RÄTSCH, CHRISTIAN: *Pflanzen der Liebe.* Hallwag Verlag, Bern and Stuttgart, 1990.

REKO, V. A.: *Magische Gifte.* Ferdinand Enke Verlag, Stuttgart, 1949.

RUÍZ, H. and PAVON, J.: "Flora Peruviana, et Chilensis, sive descriptiones et Icones Plantarum Peruvianarum et Chilensium"; *segunda systema Linnaeanum digestae, cum characteribus Plurium generum evulgatorum reformatis. Vol. 2:* 15, 1799.

SAFFORD, W. E.: "Synopsis of the genus *Datura.*" *Journal of the Washington Academy of Sciences* 11(8): 173–189, 1921.

SAFFORD, W. E.: "*Daturas* of the Old World and New: an account of their narcotic properties and their use in oracular and initiatory ceremonies." *Annual Report Smithsonian Institute,* 1920: 537–567, 1922.

SCHLEIFFER, H.: *Narcotic Plants of the Old World.* Lubrecht & Cramer, Monticello, N.Y., 1979.

SCHULTES, R. E.: "A new narcotic genus from the Amazon slope of the Colombian Andes." *Botanical Museum Leaflets,* Harvard Univ. 17(1): 1–11, 1955.

SCHULTES, R. E. and HOFMANN, A.: *The Botany and Chemistry of Hallucinogens.* Ch. C. Thomas, Springfield, Illinois, 1980.

SCHULTES, R. E. and HOFMANN, A. H.: *Pflanzen der Götter,* Hallwag Verlag, Bern, 1980.

SCHULTES, R. E. and RAFFAUF, R. F. L.: *The Healing Forest*. Dioscorides Press, Portland, Oregon, 1990.

SCHULTES R. E. and RAFFAUF, R. F.: "Phytochemical and Ethnopharmacological Notes on the Solanaceae of the Northwest Amazon." In: *Solanaceae III. Royal Botanic Gardens Kew and Linnean Society of London*: 25–51, 1991.

SIEBER, A. and VOSS, A. (Publ): *Vilmorin's Blumengärtnerei*. P. Parey, Berlin: 726–729, 1896.

SYMON, DAVID, E. and HAEGI, LAURENCE A. R.: "*Datura* (solanaceae) is a New World Genus." In: *Solanaceae III. Royal Botanic Gardens Kew and Linnean Society of London*: 197–210. 1991.

TROLL, W.: *Vergleichende Morphologie der höheren Pflanzen. 3 Bände*. Verlag Gebrüder Borntraeger, Berlin, 1935/1939/1943.

TSCHUDI, J. J. v.: "Peru: Reiseskizzen aus den Jahren 1838–1842." *Verlag v. Scheitlin u. Zollikofer, St. Gallen*: 21–23, 1846.

VAN STEENIS, C. G. G. J.: "*Brugmansia* or *Pseudodatura*?" *Bulletin Jardin Botanique Buitenzorg III*. 11(1): 15–18, 1930.

VAN ZIJP, C.: "Pseudo*datura*" nov. gen. *Tijdschrift Voor De Wif-en Natuurkundige Wetenschappen* 80: 24–28, 1920.

WETTSTEIN, R. v.: "Solanaceae." In: Engler, A. u. Prantl, K.: Die natürlichen Pflanzenfamilien. IV. *Teil*. Verlag Wilhelm Engelmann, Leipzig. 1897.

Below: *Brugmansia* hybrid 'Charles Grimaldi', description page 91.

140

Sources

The importation of live plants and plant materials across borders requires special arrangements, which will be detailed in suppliers' catalogs. Please note also that due to the poisonous nature of *Brugmansia* and *Datura*, there may be additional restrictions regarding their importation or shipment.

American regulations vary according to the country of origin and type of plant. Every order requires a phytosanitary certificate and may require a CITES (Convention on International Trade in Endangered Species of Wild Fauna and Flora) certificate. For more information contact:
USDA-APHIS-PPQ
Permit Unit
4700 River Road, Unit 136
Riverdale, Maryland 20727-1236
Tel: (301) 734-8645
Fax: (301) 734-5786
Website: www.aphis.udsda.gov

Canadians importing plant material must pay a fee and complete an "application for permit to import." Contact:
Plant Health and Production Division
Canadian Food Inspection Agency
2nd Floor West, Permit Office
59 Camelot Drive
Nepean, Ontario K1A 0Y9
Tel: (613) 225-2342
Fax: (613) 228-6605
Website: www.cfia-agr.ca

B and T World Seeds
Paguignan
34210 Olonzac, France
Tel: ++33 04 68 91 30 39
Fax: ++33 04 68 91 29 63
Website: www.b-and-t-world-seeds.com
E-mail: m@b-and-t-world-seeds.com
Large selection of seeds shipped around the world. Catalog can be downloaded from their website.

Heronswood Nursery, Ltd.
7530 NE 288th Street
Kingston, Washington 98346
Tel: (360) 297-4172
Fax: (360) 297-8321
Website: www.heronswood.com
Selection of *Brugmansia* plants.

Le Bon Jardinier
1341 N. Trigonia Road
Greenback, Tennessee 37742
Tel: (865) 856-5446
Website: www.lebonjardinier.com
E-mail: jardinier@att.net
Wide selection of seeds and plants. Does not ship live plants outside of the United States.

Logee's Greenhouses Ltd.
141 North Street
Danielson, Connecticut 06239-1939
Tel: (860) 774-8038
Toll-free Tel: (888) 330-8038
Toll-free Fax: (888)774-9932
Website: www.logees.com
Catalogs available online and by mail.

Native Habitat Ethnobotanicals
PO Box 644023
Vero Beach, Florida 32964-4023
Tel/Fax: (561) 778-8361
Website: www.nativehabitat.com
Large selection of *Datura* and *Brugmansia*, including Mehrfacht Hybrids.

Pure Land Ethnobotanicals
2701 University Avenue, PMB 463
Madison, Wisconsin 53705-3700
Fax: (801) 729-0982
Toll-free Fax: (800) 848-5198 (U.S. only)
Website: ethnobotanicals.com
E-mail: info@ethnobotanicals.com
Wide variety of *Datura* and *Brugmansia* seeds.

Richters
357 Highway 47
Goodwood, Ontario L0C 1A0
Tel: (905) 640-6677
Fax: (905) 640-6641
Website: www.richters.com
Specializes in herbs but does carry *Datura* and *Brugmansia* seeds and plants. Ships to the United States.

Seedman.com
3421 Bream Street
Gautier, Missouri 39553
Tel: (228) 497-6544
Toll-free Tel: (800) 336-2064 (orders, U.S. only)
Fax: (228) 497-5488
Website: www.seedman.com
E-mail: seedman@datasync.com
Wide variety of seeds.

William Dam Seeds Ltd.
Box 8400
Dundas, Ontario L9H 6M1
Tel: (905) 628-6641
Fax: (905) 627-1729
Website: www.williamdam.com
Ships to the United States.

Index

Figures with asterisks indicate major points in the text, numbers in bold indicate photographs or illustrations.